Siri™
FOR
DUMMIES®

006.
.5
SAL

Siri for dummies
047284

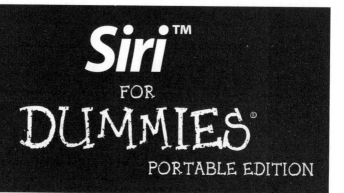

Siri™
FOR
DUMMIES®
PORTABLE EDITION

by Marc Saltzman

WILEY

John Wiley & Sons, Inc.

Siri™ For Dummies®, Portable Edition

Published by
John Wiley & Sons, Inc.
111 River Street
Hoboken, NJ 07030-5774
www.wiley.com

WILEY

About the Author

Marc Saltzman is a prolific journalist, author, and TV/radio personality specializing in consumer electronics, Internet trends, and interactive entertainment.

While *Siri For Dummies* is his first book for John Wiley & Sons, Inc., Marc has authored 15 books since 1996, covering topics such as video games, apps, mobility, and movies.

Along with his syndicated column with Gannett, Marc currently contributes to nearly 50 high-profile publications and online resources in North America, including *USA Today,* AARP, MSN, Yahoo!, *Costco Connection,* Common Sense Media, *Toronto Star,* Postmedia, Media Planet, and Sympatico.

Marc hosts a number of video segments, including "Games and Gadgets" (a weekly spot on CNN) and "Gear Guide" (seen at Cineplex movie theaters and sister chains across Canada) and is a regular guest on CNN International, Daily Buzz, and CTV's Canada AM. Marc also hosts "Tech Talk," a syndicated radio spot across Canada.

Follow Marc on Twitter (@marc_saltzman) and Facebook (www.facebook.com/marc.saltzman).

Dedication

This book is dedicated to my beautiful wife, Kellie, and my three awesome kids: Maya, Jacob, and Ethan. Thanks for letting me talk, joke, and argue with Siri — and for not calling the people with the white jackets to take me away.

Acknowledgments

Allow me to take this opportunity to thank all the fine folks at John Wiley & Sons, Inc., for their knowledge (hardly *Dummies*), professionalism, and support. I'd also like to acknowledge the overworked yet often underappreciated public relations team at Apple, Inc.

Publisher's Acknowledgments

We're proud of this book; please send us your comments at http://dummies.custhelp.com. For other comments, please contact our Customer Care Department within the U.S. at 877-762-2974, outside the U.S. at 317-572-3993, or fax 317-572-4002.

Some of the people who helped bring this book to market include the following:

Acquisitions and Editorial

Senior Project Editor: Paul Levesque

Acquisitions Editor: Kyle Looper

Copy Editor: Heidi Unger

Technical Editor: Dennis Cohen

Editorial Manager: Leah Michael

Editorial Assistant: Amanda Graham

Senior Editorial Assistant: Cherie Case

Cartoons: Rich Tennant
(www.the5thwave.com)

Composition Services

Senior Project Coordinator: Kristie Rees

Layout and Graphics: Melanee Habig, Lavonne Roberts

Proofreaders: Shannon Ramsey, Rob Springer

Indexer:
BIM Indexing & Proofreading Services

Publishing and Editorial for Technology Dummies

Richard Swadley, Vice President and Executive Group Publisher

Andy Cummings, Vice President and Publisher

Mary Bednarek, Executive Acquisitions Director

Mary C. Corder, Editorial Director

Publishing for Consumer Dummies

Kathleen Nebenhaus, Vice President and Executive Publisher

Composition Services

Debbie Stailey, Director of Composition Services

Contents at a Glance

Table of Contents

Introduction

I'm thrilled to present you with *Siri For Dummies,* your definitive guide to unlocking the power of your iPhone's voice-activated personal assistant.

Throughout these chapters, you'll find out how to take full advantage of Siri's awesome abilities — in a language you can understand. Yes, you can put away your geek-to-English dictionary, as you won't need it here.

Siri For Dummies covers all the things you can do on the iPhone 4S — via your voice — ranging from productivity and connectivity features to information, calculation, and navigation. And of course, you'll see examples of the various responses you can expect through Siri.

About This Book

This book was meant to be read in any order. Sure, you can flip through it from beginning to end if you prefer a more linear read, starting with the introduction on what Siri is, its history, and how to use this remarkable tool. Alternatively, you can jump from chapter and chapter if one topic interests you more than another.

Each chapter can stand on its own, so you won't miss anything by reading out of order. (Aren't you a rebel.)

Of course, individual chapters focus on something specific Siri can do — such as transcribing your e-mails or finding a good Italian restaurant — with clear, step-by-step instructions on how to get the best results from your voice commands.

Because Siri is so versatile, you can often ask or instruct Siri to perform tasks in different ways than I've highlighted — not to mention the fact that you just might get a different response. The idea here is that you can use this book as a loose guide if you feel like experimenting with Siri's abilities or stick to the same phrasing as I used. It's really your call.

I'll also suggest ways to get what you need from Siri in the shortest number of steps, but you might prefer a more back-and-forth exchange with Siri if you're in the mood for a conversation. Hey, we all get bored or lonely at times, and so Siri can keep you company with small talk, stories, and cheeky comebacks to your requests.

Just as sections of this book are divided by individual task, there are a few subtopics within each chapter. For example, Chapter 5 is on how Siri can get you information you may need — but this chapter is broken up into definitions, fast facts, mathematical equations, stock and currency info, and voice-driven web searches. You get the idea.

In some cases, I cross-reference subjects with topics from other chapters when relevant, but you can ignore them if you like.

How to Use This Book

Consider *Siri For Dummies* a reference book. Therefore, you can start by thumbing through the specific topics in the Table of Contents and then go to a particular chapter that interests you.

While the book is meant to be informative, you'll find the tone conversational. The only exception is the step-by-step instructions on performing the tasks in question. That is, when talking with friends in person I don't typically say things like, "Step 1 is to press such and such; Step 2 is to say this and that," and so on — but a *For Dummies* book helps by outlining the necessary steps required to perform actions.

Keep in mind that you'll probably benefit most from this book if you keep your iPhone 4S on hand while reading. That way, you can try out all of Siri's features on the spot.

What You Can Safely Ignore

When you come across a section within a chapter that contains the steps you need to take to get something done, you can disregard all text accompanying each step (the text that isn't in **bold**) if you're tight on time or don't want to read through more material. I won't be offended, really. Take what you need and ignore the rest.

As much as possible, I've also added various tips and tricks to getting the most out of Siri, along with a handful of optional "didya know?" tidbits. For example, Siri wasn't designed to let you update Twitter or Facebook using your voice, but I discovered a smart way around it.

But you don't need to wade through these factoids or ancillary abilities of Siri if you prefer to stick to the basics. Most of these extra paragraphs are labeled as Technical Stuff or Tip (see the "Icons Used in This Book" section). Then again, you might be more interested in these "sides" than the main course. (I'm sometimes like that when I visit my favorite deli.)

If you're more interested in finding out how Siri can help you remain productive when you do all the serious things you need to do on a day-to-day basis, you can also safely ignore Chapter 7, which focuses on fun and quirky things you can ask or say to Siri.

Also note there are a lot of screen captures in this book. After all, *Siri For Dummies* is all about what you can say to your iPhone 4S and what Siri will do, say, or display in response. Therefore, I wanted to show you as much visual information as possible, whether you have your iPhone 4S nearby or not.

Foolish Assumptions

I'll make only two major assumptions: You own an iPhone 4S and want to know how to get the most out of Siri.

By the time you read this book, however, Siri might be a feature in other Apple products — such as the iPad 3, iPhone 5, the next-generation iPod touch, and maybe even Mac-based computers or television products. So while I focus exclusively on the iPhone 4S, expect to see Siri expand to other products over the coming months and years.

And as I make clear in the very next chapter, this is just the beginning of Siri. This voice-activated personal assistant will expand its abilities over time, too, so don't assume this is all

Siri can do! The best, as they say, is yet to come. But this book covers everything you need to know right now.

 Siri isn't available as a download for non-4S iPhones. That is, you might be the proud owner of an iPhone 4 or 3GS (or maybe an iPod touch or iPad), but despite a few hacks you might read about online, there's no official Siri for devices outside of iPhone 4S. Plus, you might've already sampled the Voice Control feature on previous iPhones or iPod touches, which let you control your music with your voice. This is also folded into Siri, but is just a fraction of what your new personal assistant can do.

Icons Used in This Book

The following icons are placed in the margins of the book's pages to point out stuff you may or may not want to read.

 This icon warns you of geeky descriptions or explanations you may want to pass on — but don't expect a lot of this throughout this easy-to-read handbook.

 This icon offers suggestions to enhancing your experience. Most are tied to the topic at hand, while others are more general in nature.

 This icon reminds you of important information related to Siri. This info might've been covered previously in the book, but I thought it would be a good idea to refresh your memory.

 Siri can be a powerful tool to getting information or getting things done, but this icon alerts you to important considerations when using Siri — including health, safety, or security concerns.

Where to Go from Here

If you've never used an iPhone 4S before — perhaps you purchased this book in anticipation of buying one or receiving the phone as a gift — it might be best to become familiar with the basic features of your device before having Siri perform tasks for you.

For example, you might try to interact with your iPhone's Calendar app — with your fingertips — before turning to Siri to help you out. Not only will you gain a better understanding of what Siri is doing for you, but you'll also gain a deeper appreciation of how Siri can speed up and simplify these tasks!

Well, that's about it. As you can see, you don't need much to begin reading *Siri For Dummies* — just a desire to save time and aggravation while using your iPhone 4S. And as you'll see with the final chapter, a sense of humor doesn't hurt either.

Chapter 1

Getting to Know Siri

● ●

In This Chapter

▶ Seeing what — or rather, who — Siri is

▶ Setting up Siri for your personal use

▶ Exploring different ways to use Siri

▶ Finding out how to get fast and reliable replies

▶ Teaching Siri what to call you

● ●

*C*ongratulations! You're now the owner of the most definitive guide to Siri on the planet.

This easy-to-read *For Dummies* title will teach you everything
you need to know about Siri — and then some. Be prepared to
master all of Siri's amazing features, at your own pace, so you
can get a lot more out of your beloved iPhone 4S. But first, a
few words about my introduction to Siri, what Siri is exactly,
and a bit of history.

As a longtime technology reviewer, I firmly believe Siri (pro-
nounced *SEAR-ree*) is the start of something very special, and
it was love at first sight — er, speech.

Here I am, sitting in the crowd at Apple's headquarters in
Cupertino, California, on October 4, 2011. The exclusive press
event is called "Let's Talk iPhone," and like many other jour-
nalists and analysts in the room, I was expecting Apple's CEO
Tim Cook to take the wraps off the iPhone 5.

When the iPhone 4S was initially debuted, you could sense the
initial disappointment among the attendees — after all, there
were so many rumors leading up to the event that it seemed
inevitable that a dramatically new smartphone would be
unveiled that day.

But that letdown feeling completely vanished the moment Siri was introduced. Forget the iPhone 4S's faster processor, better camera, built-in support for the iOS 5 operating system and Apple's iCloud — the service that wirelessly synchronizes all your content between devices— it was Siri that truly held the magic that the late, great Steve Jobs often spoke of. (You may recall Jobs, Apple's visionary leader, passed away the following day, on October 5, at age 56.)

I knew right then and there, while at the Apple campus, that Siri would usher in a new and exciting way to interact with our mobile devices. I was so blown away by Siri that I e-mailed my book contacts on the spot, because I just had to be part of this revolutionary technology — and explaining to others how to best use Siri seemed like a fitting role given my effort to translate "geek speak into street speak" in my articles and TV and radio appearances.

Siri might be exclusive to the iPhone 4S at the time of this writing, but it could very well play a major role in the next generation of iPad tablets and iPod touch devices, and perhaps other Apple products, including Macs and Apple TV.

So What is Siri, Anyway?

Siri can best be described as a personal assistant that resides on your iPhone 4S, all controlled by your voice instead of your fingertips.

In other words, Siri was built for talking rather than typing. And it goes both ways: Just as you can talk to your iPhone 4S to perform a range of tasks (employing speech-to-text translation), you'll also hear Siri's human-like voice talk back at you (text-to-speech technology).

Aha, so that's why "Let's Talk iPhone" was the name for Apple's iPhone 4S unveiling.

Think of Siri as being both software and a service, since all of your questions and commands are instantly uploaded to Siri's secure servers, and the appropriate actions and responses are sent back down to the iPhone.

Apple doesn't often pull back the ⟨
but here's how the company expla
FAQ (Frequently Asked Questions

Siri uses the processing power of t
4S, and it uses 3G and Wi-Fi netwc.
with Apple's data centers. So it can quickly understand ...
say and what you're asking for, then quickly return a response.

Using your voice, Siri can help you perform a number of tasks
on your iPhone 4S much faster than if you typed them. Such
tasks include things like:

- Sending e-mails and text messages
- Finding specific messages in your inbox
- Having your texts read to you — and you can reply verbally, too, and your words are transcribed back into text
- Using the built-in Wolfram|Alpha database to quickly
find useful information, such as dictionary definitions,
mathematical equations, measurement conversions, or
even fast facts and pop culture references
- Searching the web for anything and everything, including
info and media (such as photos and videos)
- Posting updates to Facebook and Twitter
- Adding and accessing calendar appointments, alarms,
timers, and reminders (Figure 1-1 shows an example of
Siri doing just that.)
- Making and accessing notes
- Getting directions from point A to point B, using the
iPhone 4S's GPS radio
- Finding businesses nearby — including directions on
getting there — be it gas stations, banks, or restaurants;
many businesses are also displayed by rating
- Making phone calls and FaceTime video calls
- Getting real-time information on weather, stock quotes,
and much more
- Accessing music and podcasts using your voice, includ-
ing the ability to control audio playback

Figure 1-1: Go ahead and give Siri a task, such as a reminder about an important date.

Whew! And that's just the start. To get a taste of what Siri can do, be sure to watch the official Apple video on Siri at www.apple.com/iphone/features/siri.html.

In fact, did you know Siri is still currently in *beta,* meaning Apple is still tweaking the software and service? That's right; as awesome as Siri is, it's not a final product. You can just imagine where Siri will go in the coming months and years.

Unlike other speech-to-text technology, including those offered by other smartphones, Siri works on the operating system level and knows which app to open based on your request. (Most other smartphone solutions require you to first open up an app before you speak.) Using advanced artificial intelligence (AI), Siri makes connections based on your relationships, uses humor to make you smile, and is eager to learn more about your world and how to make your life easier to manage.

It's interesting that, just as Apple brought the mouse to the mainstream in 1984, changing the way we used keyboard-centric personal computers, they changed the game again by bringing a comfortable touch interface to the masses in the 2000s with the iPod, iPhone, and iPad. Now, Apple is making technological history yet again by bringing a speech-based user interface to the masses — arguably the most intuitive way to interact with computers to date.

And as we saw with Captain Kirk aboard the U.S.S. Enterprise in *Star Trek*, talking with computers and getting a humanlike response is the future. Let's just hope the computers don't turn on us like they did in *2001: A Space Odyssey*; *I, Robot*; or *The Terminator*.

Spend just a few minutes with Siri and you'll no doubt fall for its charm.

A Bit o' Background

Before I get into setting up Siri, you might be interested to learn just a tad about its history.

Siri is the result of more than 40 years of research funded by DARPA (the Defense Advanced Research Projects Agency). Much of the work has been carried out at SRI International's Artificial Intelligence Center, founded in 1966. (SRI, for those not in the know, stands for Stanford Research Institute.)

Fast forward to 2007, when the company Siri (named, obviously enough, after SRI, the place of its birth) was founded by Dag Kittlaus, Adam Cheyer, and Tom Gruber, along with Norman Winarsky from SRI International's venture group. After a couple of successful rounds of financing, the company released an iOS app for iPhone, also called Siri, with plans to make it available for BlackBerry and Android devices, too.

That's right; seasoned iPhone users might recall Siri was a downloadable app at the iTunes App Store a couple of years ago. But the company was acquired by Apple Inc. in April 2010, and the app was pulled from the App Store — because of Apple's more ambitious plans for its future.

Siri's official release date as an exclusive iPhone 4S feature began on October 15, 2011, in the United States.

Also benefitting from speech-recognition technology licensed from Nuance (of Dragon NaturallySpeaking fame), Siri is also integrated with services such as Yelp, OpenTable, Google Maps, Taxi Magic, and MovieTickets.com, to name a few.

Setting up Siri

Okay, before you dive into Siri's many features — covered in depth from Chapters 2 through 7 — here's a quick primer on setting up Siri properly.

First things first: Siri is automatically built into the iPhone 4S, so you don't need to download anything to get going. When you turn on the iPhone 4S for the first time, you're prompted to set up a few things, such as enabling location information and using Siri, so be sure to choose Yes to these options.

By the way, you can always access Siri's settings in the Settings area of your iPhone 4S (tap Settings➪General➪Siri) if you need to make some changes. Figure 1-2 shows you the kinds of settings you can change for Siri.

Figure 1-2: Siri will open up your Calendar and add your requested appointment.

The first time you set up Siri, you're prompted to select the language you prefer. Your options are English (United States), English (Australia), English (United Kingdom), French, and German. (See Figure 1-3.)

But this isn't just so Siri can speak in a language you understand — it's also to let your new personal assistant

better understand you. For example, someone from the
U.S. or Canada will say "Call mom" differently than an
English-speaking person from the United Kingdom or
Australia. One might sound more like "Coll mum" or "Cull
mam," and so on.

Sure, Americans have various accents, too — there are defi-
nitely subtle differences between those from Long Island,
Boston, Dallas, or Minneapolis, for example — but American
English can be vastly different from the English spoken in
London or Sydney. So be sure to choose the correct language
from the list or you may have some difficulties understanding
Siri — and vice-versa.

Figure 1-3: It's important to select what language you need Siri to speak
(and listen for).

It's also important to note Siri has a female voice in the U.S.,
but that might not be the case with other countries (such as
the U.K., where Siri has a male voice).

For this reason, I usually refer to Siri as "it" for the majority
of this book to keep it universal, but I might refer to Siri as a
"she" from time to time, especially in the last chapter, which
focuses on all the fun things you can say to Siri and things
"she" will say back.

Okay, so we've covered the importance of choosing the right Siri voice from the list of available options, based on what language you speak and where you live.

Here are some other choices you have in Siri's settings:

- ✔ **Voice Feedback:** You can select whether you'd like to always hear Siri talk to you through the iPhone 4S speaker (which might be heard by those nearby) or only when using a hands-free option, such as a Bluetooth headset. If you simply want to read Siri's responses instead of hearing them, select "Hands-free Only" and don't use a hands-free product

- ✔ **My Info:** Here's where you'd want to list your name and contact information. You can tell Siri to call you something else, if you like (for example, a nickname), but this area points to your info in Contacts. For example, you can tell Siri, "Take me home," but she'll need to know where "home" is.

- ✔ **Raise to Speak:** The last option you have when it comes to using Siri is whether you want to set it up so that you always have to press and hold the Home button to speak to Siri or if you'd like to also enable the Raise to Speak option, which automatically lets you talk to Siri whenever you raise your phone to your ear — meaning you don't have to press the Home button.

Since the Raise to Speak option isn't going to be everyone's choice, I'm going to assume for the rest of this book that you aren't using that particular feature when I provide instruction on using Siri. I'll always start each task with the standard "Press and hold the Home button" line, but if you choose to use the Raise to Speak option, you can ignore that bit and simply raise the iPhone 4S to your ear instead.

The only other option you'll have to worry about for Siri is in the Passcode section (under Settings⇨General). You can choose to use Siri even if your phone is locked (and requires a four-digit PIN) or you might opt to always force yourself to unlock your phone before you can use Siri. The advantage to using Siri when locked is you'll get your information faster — because you don't have to type in a code first to unlock the phone. On the flipside, allowing Siri to be used without unlocking the phone means if you lose your iPhone 4S (or if it's stolen), someone can potentially access information on your phone by asking Siri the right questions. It's your call, but remember this is an option that comes with pros and cons.

Talking to Siri

To talk to Siri, you'll simply press down on the Home button (that small circle at the bottom of your iPhone 4S), wait until you hear a short chime that sounds like two quick beeps, and then talk away.

 You'll also see a purple-tinged microphone icon on the lower portion of the screen. You'll know that Siri is listening to you speak because you'll see a lighted ring rotate around the microphone icon. (Figure 1-4 gives you an idea of what I mean, even if I can't recreate the rotating ring business.)

Figure 1-4: Get used to seeing that little purple microphone. This means you're chatting with Siri.

When you ask Siri a question — such as, "What's the weather like in Seattle tomorrow?" — you can stop talking after you're done and you'll hear a beep to confirm Siri is now processing your request.

Alternatively, you can tap the microphone icon when you're done speaking, which might be a bit faster than Siri waiting for silence to begin the request.

The next thing you'll see is your words spoken to Siri, in bold, near the top of the iPhone 4S screen. This confirms to you that Siri understands what you're saying or asking.

If you make a mistake while asking Siri a question (maybe you accidentally said the wrong person's name to text) or perhaps Siri didn't hear you clearly, you can tap the microphone icon to let Siri know you want to cancel the request. After a second or two, you can tap it again and start over. You'll hear the familiar tone and see the ring rotate around the microphone icon to confirm Siri is listening for your new request.

The final thing you'll see is when Siri performs your desired action. Siri might open up a map, an e-mail message, calendar entry, or restaurant listing. Depending on the task, Siri might also speak to you with the information you seek. With the weather, for example, you'll see and hear the answer, but if it's a dictionary definition or numerical equation, Siri might say something like, "Here you go" or "This might answer your question" and show you the information on the screen.

Because all requests to Siri are uploaded to a server, it's not unheard of for the server to be temporarily inaccessible — if the first couple of months of using Siri is any indication. Siri will apologize to you and ask that you please try again later. A problem with Siri *isn't* an indication that there's a problem with your phone, so don't fret. The outage is usually only a couple of minutes (if that), but it's something you should be aware of.

Keeping the lines of communication open

This section gets into how you can up your success rate when it comes to using Siri, which comes down to making sure it understands what you're saying so that it can come back with quick and accurate results.

The first thing to remember is you need to have a wireless Internet connection to perform all tasks — even if it's a local task such as asking Siri to jot down a shopping list in your

Notes app. Whether it's a cellular signal you're using (make sure you see a few bars on the top-left of your phone) or Wi-Fi (a wireless network), you'll need decent reception to get quick results from Siri. This is critical.

Secondly, you'll want to speak clearly — I know this can be difficult to be conscious of — but the less you mumble and more you articulate your words, the better Siri works. Don't worry; Siri is remarkably keen on picking up what you say (and even what you mean) so you don't need to speak like a robot. Just be aware you'll get better results with clearer speech.

Also be aware that a lot of background noise isn't great for Siri, as it might not be able to pick up what you're saying very well. The quieter the environment, the better Siri can understand your instructions. This might be tough if you're in a crowded restaurant or walking down a busy street, of course, so you might need to speak a little bit louder and closer to the iPhone 4S microphone.

 Hands down, Siri is the most exciting thing to happen to the iPhone — but be aware that this new technology uses up quite a bit of data to function. As a result, make sure you have a good data plan with your cellular provider so you don't go over your monthly allowance. (You'll likely get a warning if you get close.) Also, using Siri can affect battery performance of the iPhone 4S, therefore you may need to charge up your phone every evening. Some "power users" — if you can pardon the pun — invest in a battery pack that keeps the iPhone 4S topped up all day long.

You can call me Al

Siri refers to you by your name — sometimes you'll see it written, and in some cases you might hear it spoken aloud by Siri. But did you know that you can change what Siri calls you? That's right, at any time you can tell Siri what you'd prefer to be called, and your request will be granted.

Here's what to do:

1. **Press and hold the Home button.**

   The little chime you hear means Siri is listening for your request.

2. Tell Siri something like, "Call me Dude."

Siri will then say something like, "Okay, from now on I will call you Dude." You can tap Yes or Cancel. See Figure 1-5 for what you'd see on your iPhone 4S screen.

Figure 1-5: You can ask Siri to call you something else, if you like.

Going forward, when Siri addresses you personally, you'll see and hear "Dude" instead of your real name, as you'll see in Figure 1-6. Need I mention that it's okay to have fun with Siri? It feels good.

As you'll soon find out with the help of this fine book you're holding, you can also tell Siri who the important people are in your life, such as, "My mom is Honey" (yes, that's my mom's real name!), "My dad is Stan," and "My wife is Kellie," and Siri remembers all of this. Now you can say things like, "Text my dad," "E-mail my mom," "Call my wife," and so on. Go ahead and tell Siri important relationships, as well as key dates like birthdays and anniversaries, too.

Okay, now that you've nailed the basics, you're ready to tackle *Siri For Dummies* in any order you like. Feel free to jump around or simply swipe to the next page to begin with Chapter 2, which is all about getting organized — including using Siri for calendars, reminders, notes, alarms, timers, and more. Much, much more.

310-410 📶   2:27 PM

What can I help you with?

" Hi Siri how are you "

I'm fine, Dude. Thanks for asking.

Figure 1-6: Change your name to whatever you like, and Siri will call you that — until told otherwise.

"The Beta Test Initiation"

Siri has already been immortalized in pop culture, thanks to a tribute by the cast of *The Big Bang Theory*. Starring four socially awkward friends — two physicists, an aerospace engineer, and an astrophysicist — the hit CBS sitcom devoted an episode to the female-sounding personal assistant in its January 26, 2012 episode. The character Rajesh Koothrappali (played by Kunal Nayyar), who is unable to talk to women unless he's inebriated, romantically bonds with Siri and even comes face to face with the woman behind the voice. It's a hilarious episode (number 101 in the TV series), so be sure to watch it!

Chapter 2

Using Siri to Organize Your Life

*I*n Chapter 1, you find out about some of the amazing things Siri can do for you — at a high level. Time now to take a deeper dive into some of the ways Siri can help you stay organized and informed, wherever life takes you.

Specifically, Siri can seriously speed up common — and often mundane — tasks, such as adding entries to a calendar, setting a reminder to do something, making notes, and setting alarms.

Menial tasks that often take multiple steps when typing can be performed in mere seconds — with great accuracy — when you get to use your voice.

Siri is the key, and so without further ado, I cover how to take advantage of your voice-activated personal assistant to get more done in less time.

Keeping a Calendar

Whether you rely on your smartphone personally or professionally (or, in all likelihood, a little bit of both), your trusty handheld device can definitely help you stay organized while on the go.

After all, unlike a paper day timer (if you remember those!), your smartphone can alert you to important meetings, wirelessly synchronize this information with other devices, and also let you easily search for entries by keyword.

Siri goes one step further by making it drop-dead simple to add or access calendar entries — without having to stop to manually type in all the information.

To minimize redundancy, be sure to take advantage of Apple's iCloud service, which wirelessly synchronizes all your information and content between multiple devices (up to 5GB for free). Your calendar entries automatically sync with your personal computer or other iOS device (such as an iPad or iPod touch). When you add or edit an entry on your iPhone 4S, tablet, or computer, all devices are updated over the Internet. To set up calendar entries with iCloud, go to Settings on your iPhone, tap iCloud, and swipe to turn on Calendars (underneath Contacts).

Adding new calendar entries

Adding a new calendar appointment using Siri is a breeze.

1. **Press and hold the Home button.**

   The little chime you hear means Siri is listening for your instructions.

2. **Tell Siri about a calendar appointment you'd like to make.**

   For example, say, "Remember to call Auntie Terry-Lynn at 5pm tomorrow" or "Set up a meeting about the sales report at 9 a.m. Thursday." (Figure 2-1 shows what a Meet-Wife-at-Noon request to Siri looks like.)

Figure 2-1: Siri will open up your Calendar and add your requested appointment.

3. Confirm or cancel the appointment.

Say "Cancel" or "Yes" —— or tap Cancel or Confirm — to either cancel or confirm the appointment.

Siri might warn you that your proposed appointment overlaps with an existing one. (See Figure 2-2.) Or Siri might ask you to confirm the person you want the meeting with (this could happen if you say, "John," for example, and there are nine people named John in your Contacts). If you say or tap Cancel, Siri will stamp a red CANCELED notification across the screen, and you might see some words like "All right, I'll leave it off your calendar."

Siri isn't too picky: You can ask Siri to set up an appointment in a number of different ways. You can say, "Add calendar entry," "New appointment with *person*," "Set up a meeting," or "Meet with *person*," to name a few examples.

Figure 2-2: If there's a calendar appointment overlap, Siri will warn you about it.

Adding a new calendar entry — with location information

Along with the date and time, you can also use Siri to set a location for your appointment.

1. **Press and hold the Home button.**

2. **Give Siri a calendar-related command.**

   Say something like, "Schedule a sales meeting tomorrow at 9 a.m. in the boardroom."

3. **Review what Siri is showing you.**

   Preview the calendar entry — time, subject, and place — before accepting the appointment. The location for the meeting displays underneath the subject, as shown in Figure 2-3.

   After Siri shows you the confirmed calendar appointment, you can tap the entry and it'll open up the Calendar app for you to add or edit details, if desired. Or maybe someone walked into the room and you'd rather type discreetly than talk out loud. Simply tap the

Edit button, and you can make all kinds of alterations, including when the meeting starts and ends, the time zone, alerts and repeats, related websites, and notes. You can also delete the event from here, too. Just be aware you can edit your spoken calendar entry with typed words, if you like.

Figure 2-3: In this calendar entry, you see where the meeting is to be held ("boardroom").

Making changes to calendar appointments

Siri can do more than just create a new appointment. You can also use Siri to review and change calendar appointments.

The following are a few examples of what you can say to Siri to change or cancel appointments when you're on the run. It'll be much faster than doing these tasks yourself!

✔ **Change an appointment.** You can instruct Siri to do this for you. For example, tell Siri, "Move my 3:30 p.m. meeting to 4:30 p.m." (See Figure 2-4.) You can also say, "Reschedule my appointment at 3:30 p.m. to next Tuesday at 1:30 p.m."

Figure 2-4: It's easy as pie to change an existing appointment to another time.

✔ **Cancel a calendar appointment.** Tell Siri something like, "Cancel my 12 p.m. lunch meeting with Julie." Or if you want to feel important — like those rich CEOs in the movies — you can even say something like, "Cancel my 1 o'clock!," and Siri will ask you if you want to cancel the calendar appointment for that time. Have your people call my people.

✔ **Add someone to an existing calendar appointment.** For example, tell Siri, "Add Mary Smith to my meeting at 3:30 p.m." (Figure 2-5 shows you how Siri complies with your request.)

You can use Siri even when your iPhone 4S is locked — but only if you want to. That is, by default, you can pull your phone right out of your jacket pocket or purse and press and hold the Home button to give Siri some instructions. This can save you a step as you need not unlock the phone first. But if you prefer, you can turn off this feature in the Passcode Lock settings (tap Settings⇨General⇨Passcode Lock⇨Siri).

Figure 2-5: Based on your instructions, Siri adds Mary Smith to your appointment with Mike Jones.

Reviewing calendar appointments

Siri can also help you quickly review your calendar appointments. The following bullet list highlights a few examples of what you can ask Siri and what you'll see and hear in return:

✓ **"What does my day look like?"**

Siri shows you today's calendar entries.

✓ **"When is my next meeting?"**

Siri tells and shows you the time for your next appointment.

✓ **"What do I have on Friday?" (See Figure 2-6.)**

Siri displays all calendar entries for a given date.

✓ **"When am I meeting with Julie?"**

Siri says and displays the time for your next appointment.

✓ **"Where is my meeting with Steven?"**

Siri tells you the location for the relevant appointment and shows you the calendar entry, too.

Figure 2-6: Ask Siri what's on tap and you'll see your calendar appointments.

Setting Reminders

Apple added a handy Reminders app as part of its iOS 5 update in the fall of 2011. In other words, it's included on your iPhone 4S, likely on your Home screen (the front page of all your apps). As the name suggests, this app lets you create and view quite a few reminders — without having to add them to your calendar.

This pocket-sized to-do list, if you will, makes it easy to set or view reminders. For example, when viewing reminders, there are multiple ways to organize everything you have to do — be it by date, priority, location, or any custom-made list you want to create (such as Family Stuff, Work Notes, and so on.) And of course, the Reminders app notifies you when you should do that thing you need to do.

Siri makes using Reminders a lot easier as it takes just a few seconds to instruct Siri to add a reminder to your to-do list.

Here's how to get going.

Starting a reminder

If you'd like Siri to remind you to do something in the future, take out your iPhone 4S and try the following operation.

1. **Press and hold the Home button.**

   You'll hear the familiar chime, letting you know Siri is ready for action.

2. **Tell Siri what you'd like to do.**

   Speak into your iPhone 4S with a command like, "Remind me to buy milk, bread, and eggs today at 4 p.m." or you can say something like, "Remember to thank John for the present."

3. **Glance at your iPhone 4S screen to review your reminder. Or listen to Siri's confirmation.**

4. **Assuming everything looks good to you, say or tap "Yes" to create the reminder. (If something isn't quite right, say, "Cancel," to cancel the reminder.)**

   Figure 2-7 shows you what a reminder confirmation from Siri looks like.

Figure 2-7: Here's what a typical reminder confirmation looks like — after you've approved it.

Because it takes only a quick Siri request to set up a reminder, you might be tempted to do this while driving. But even a minor distraction could cause an accident, so resist using Siri until you've parked the car.

Telling Siri when to remind you

If you tell Siri to remind you about something but don't specify a time or date, you'll be asked to do so on the spot. Neat, huh? This is how the exchange looks with Siri:

1. **Press and hold the Home button.**

   You'll know Siri is ready for instructions when you hear the familiar chime.

2. **Tell Siri what to remind you of.**

   For example, say, "Remind me to call mom."

3. **When Siri prompts you to specify a date and/or time, tell Siri when you'd like to be reminded of whatever you stated needed reminding.**

   Figure 2-8 shows you what a reminder on your iPhone 4S looks like.

Figure 2-8: If you forget to tell Siri when to be reminded, you'll be asked to set a date and time.

Setting a location for your reminder

One of the coolest things about using Siri is you can ask to be reminded to do tasks by location, too. Because the iPhone 4S is location-aware (thanks to its GPS chip), you can instruct Siri to remind you about something when you leave or arrive at a particular location.

Here's a quick step-by-step on using Siri to remind you about a task when you leave somewhere:

1. **Press and hold the Home button.**

   You'll know Siri is ready with the short beeping sound.

2. **Tell Siri to remind you about something — but at the end say, "when I leave here."**

   For example, say, "Remind me to buy flowers and wine when I leave here." (See Figure 2-9.) Another example: "Remind me to take an umbrella when I leave" (no "here" is necessary).

Figure 2-9: Siri displays your reminder request, with your geographical location info at the bottom of the reminder.

3. **Preview the reminder and if it's good, say "Yes" or "OK," or tap "Confirm."**

   You'll see your address at the bottom of the reminder. (As you can see, I took the liberty of covering up my address for privacy reasons!) When you leave this address, your iPhone 4S will remind you to pick up flowers and wine.

Now, say you want to be reminded about something when you arrive at a particular location? Here's how to use Siri to perform this handy task:

1. **Press and hold the Home button.**

   Siri tells you it's time to speak your request with the familiar chime.

2. **Tell Siri to remind you about something but add the words "when I get to *destination*."**

   For example, you can say, "Remind me to FaceTime with Mary Smith when I get home" or "Remind me to talk to John about the contract renewal when I get to the office."

3. **Siri sets the reminder — and location — and asks that you confirm the details.**

   If Siri doesn't know your home or business address, you'll be asked to fill in this information in your Contacts (and Siri will open it up for you), as shown in Figure 2-10.

You can also combine a date with a location! For example, you can tell Siri something like, "Remind me to make a doctor's appointment Monday morning when I get to the office."

Previewing your reminders

You can also ask Siri to preview your reminders. She won't read them to you verbally, but she will tell you if you have any you should know about and display them on the screen.

To preview your reminders, follow these steps:

1. **Press and hold the Home button.**

   You'll hear the Siri chime, which is your cue to begin speaking.

2. **Ask Siri if you have any reminders.**

   You can ask it in different ways, but it might be easiest to ask, "Do I have any reminders today?" Or you can ask "Do I have any reminders tomorrow?" or "Do I have any reminders next week?"

   Siri will display whatever reminders you have listed in the Reminders app for a given date or location.

As you'll see in Figure 2-11, you can ask Siri to show you reminders by location, too (in this case "at home").

While it's very fast to ask Siri to show you reminders for today, it's even faster to slide your finger down from the top of the iPhone 4S screen to open the Notifications app. Part of this screen includes upcoming reminders for the day. Also, remember that you can also turn Reminders on in the iCloud service, meaning all reminders will be synched between your iPad, iPod touch, Mac, and PC. To set this up on your iPhone 4S, tap Settings⇨iCloud⇨Reminders.

Figure 2-10: Siri didn't know my home address, so I was prompted to give it (just once).

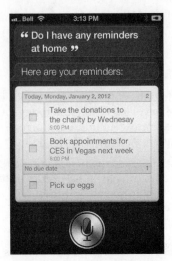

Figure 2-11: You can ask Siri to show you a list of uncompleted reminders.

Taking Notes

As with most smartphones, the iPhone 4S ships with a Notes app — all decked out to look like yellow, lined pieces of paper — allowing you to jot your thoughts down whenever they pop into your head.

The Notes app isn't a full-blown word processor — for example, there aren't multiple font styles or sizes to choose from (only one for each, in fact) — but it's an ideal tool to flesh out ideas and make lists and such. And with iCloud, Apple's handy way of synchronizing all of your digital info and media over the Internet (between supported devices), all your notes can be synched with all your devices, too.

You can, of course, manually tap to open the Notes application, start a new note, and begin typing — or you can be smart and have Siri do it for you.

You can use Siri to start a new note, add words to an existing note, and pull up notes based on keywords.

Creating a new note

Here's a look at the first task I mentioned, starting a new note:

1. **Press and hold the Home button.**

   You'll hear the familiar tone, which is your cue to begin talking.

2. **Instruct Siri to create a new note for you.**

   You can say something like, "Note that I spent $50 on the fantasy football pool," "Create a note called 'Buy these books' for mom," or "Take a note: Pick up that new Xbox 360 game for Steve."

   Siri opens up the Notes app, begins a new note with the name you've given it, and then shows you the note it just created for you. (See Figure 2-12 for an example of Siri's response when I ask her to create a note.) The first few words of your spoken note become the name for the note, but you can change that if you like.

   You won't get a chance to accept or cancel the note Siri creates for you. If you don't want to keep the note, you'll need to manually open up the Notes app and remove it. You can't delete notes using Siri.

Figure 2-12: Siri can help create notes for you on the fly.

Take note that you can ask Siri to create a note in different ways, such as saying, "Make a note about *this*," "Take a note about *that*," or just "Note that I did *this and that*."

Adding more to an existing note

Let's say you already created a note on your iPhone 4S and you want to add more to it. You can do this very easily with Siri's help. All you need to know is what the note is called (or as you'll see shortly, you can do a search by keyword), and you can add more text using your voice.

Here's how to get going:

1. **Press and hold the Home button.**

   You'll know it's time to talk after you hear the familiar chime.

2. **Tell Siri something like, "Add cereal to Shopping List note."**

   Remember, the note you're adding the extra words to must already be in your Notes app. Remember, when you start a new note, the first few words will be the title for the note.

3. **Look at the screen to see the note — and what has just been added — and, assuming it's all good, you can put the phone away.**

   See Figure 2-13 for an example.

4. **(Optional) If you need to edit the entry, tap the message, and the Notes app opens.**

As you can see in Figure 2-13, Siri won't always capitalize proper nouns ("jobs" should be capitalized in "Steve Jobs"), so you can manually change this by tapping the screen — if it bothers you at all, that is.

Finding notes

Your voice-activated personal assistant can also be used to find existing notes on your iPhone 4S.

Figure 2-13: Add more information to an existing note using Siri.

Perhaps you're looking for that grocery list while standing in your local supermarket? Or maybe you want to add more detail to your million dollar idea?

Instead of manually scrolling through all your notes, you can ask Siri to show you all relevant notes by saying a keyword — or all your notes, if you prefer.

Here's a quick guide on what to ask Siri:

1. **Press and hold the Home button.**

   You can begin talking after you hear the short chime.

2. **Either ask Siri to display all your notes or ask her to look for one in particular.**

   Tell Siri, "Show me all my notes," and you'll see a list of them, from newest to oldest, as shown in Figure 2-14. Tap a note to open one up. Alternatively, ask Siri to look for a particular note by telling her something along the lines of, "Show me 'book' notes," which will have her call up all notes containing the word "book." (See Figure 2-15.)

Figure 2-14: Siri can show you all your notes, if you ask to do so.

Figure 2-15: Here I asked Siri to show me all notes with the word "book" in them.

Setting Alarms, Clocks, and Timers

You can quickly set an alarm on the iPhone 4S by asking Siri to set it for you.

Before I show you how to do this (very) simple task, I want you to think of all the steps involved if you didn't use Siri. Say you want to be woken up tomorrow at 7 a.m. Without Siri, you'd have to open up your Clock app, tap on Alarm at the bottom of the screen, and then tap + to set a new alarm. Now you must select a time (for example, 7 a.m.) and tap Save. Geez, that's a drag, no?

With Siri, all you have to do is ask her to set an alarm at a given time. Two to three seconds at most, and you're done.

Setting an alarm

Here's the easy way to set an alarm:

1. **Press and hold the Home button.**

   You can ask to set an alarm right after you hear the chime.

2. **Say what time you want the alarm to go off.**

   For example, say, "Wake me up at 7 a.m. tomorrow." (See Figure 2-16.) Siri will show you the alarm, based on your request.

You can close this app if it's correct or swipe to turn it off if it's not.

Siri has additional alarm features that enable you to instruct Siri to do the following:

✔ **Want to take a nap?**

Tell Siri, "Wake me up in one hour."

✔ **Need to sleep in a little longer tomorrow?**

Instruct Siri to "Change my 7 a.m. alarm to 7:30 a.m."

✔ **Want to call in sick?**

Say, "Cancel my 7 a.m. alarm."

✔ **Want to remove the alarm notification altogether?**

Tell Siri, "Delete my 7 a.m. alarm."

Finding out what time it is

Siri can give you the time — locally or in another city altogether. Siri can also tell you today's date.

Figure 2-16: In this case, the alarm was previously set and turned off, so Siri turned the alarm back on for me.

Want to call a colleague's mobile phone in Hong Kong but don't want to call too late or too early? Here's what to do:

1. **Press and hold the Home button.**

   You'll hear a chime, which means Siri is ready for you to ask her a question.

2. **Ask Siri what time is it in Hong Kong.**

   Within a second or two, you'll see the exact time in Hong Kong. (See Figure 2-17 for an example.)

You can ask Siri to tell you the date today or another day (for example, "What is the date this Friday?"). Or you can ask Siri a question like, "How many days until Christmas?" and you'll see a thorough response from Siri, as shown in Figure 2-18.

Setting and adjusting timers

Finally, speaking of clocks and alarms, Siri can also be used to set a timer on your iPhone 4S.

Whether you want to know when to check the oven, leave the house to pick up the kids from a play date, or stop jogging around the neighborhood, you can easily set a timer using voice commands. It's as easy as this:

1. **Press and hold the Home button.**

   Listen for the chime and begin speaking.

2. **Instruct Siri to set a timer.**

   You can say the duration of the timer right away (see Figure 2-19) or say, "Set a timer," and Siri will ask you, "For how long?" However you set the duration, when that's done you'll see the timer start.

3. **Preview the timer information at a glance.**

4. **(Optional) Tap the timer info to make any changes.**

   You can change when the timer ends, the kind of alarm that sounds (by default it's Marimba), and if you want to pause the timer.

Figure 2-17: Siri shows you the current time in Hong Kong — and tells you it's tomorrow's date, too.

For even more fun, try these other timer-related commands with Siri:

✔ **"Show the timer."**

✔ **"Pause the timer."**

✓ "Resume the timer."

✓ "Cancel the timer."

Note: If the timer is already open on your iPhone 4S, you can simply say, "pause," "resume," or "cancel."

Figure 2-18: I asked Siri to tell me how many more days there are until Christmas, and she broke it down for me.

Figure 2-19: Don't let that roast burn in the oven! Siri can set a timer for you in a flash. All you have to do is ask.

Chapter 3

Using Siri while on the Go

*W*ithout question, Siri is the most exciting feature built into Apple's iPhone 4S — and because this smartphone is meant for portability, you bet Siri can help you when you're out on the town.

Specifically, Siri is a fast and powerful way to discover the world around you. If you need turn-by-turn directions, want to find a new restaurant, or simply want to know if you need an umbrella today, Siri can help you with all three scenarios.

This chapter helps you unlock Siri's capabilities when you're out of your home and looking to roam.

Turning to Siri for Navigation

Because the iPhone 4S has built-in GPS technology, it can communicate with satellites that hover above the planet and help pinpoint your location on earth. When paired with the Maps application on the phone, you can use it to get where you need to go — simply by asking Siri to help.

e not as powerful as standalone GPS navigation units
speak to you (or downloadable GPS apps for iPhone like
Tom or Navigon, for that matter), it's very convenient for
to take you to a particular location. (Along with giving you
audio-based turn-by-turn directions, standalone GPS units and
dedicated GPS apps have more advanced navigation features —
such as large arrows that show you what lane to get into on the
freeway — than the bundled Maps application on the iPhone.)

In fact, you don't need to manually type in the address you
want to travel to. With Siri, you can use your voice to get
directions to a particular location and, within seconds you'll
see where to go, how to get there, and how long it might take.

The next sections show you a few ways to pull it off.

Using Siri to find an address

Unlike most GPS units, where you need to type in the state,
city, and address of the place you want to go to, your iPhone
4S offers a voice-activated personal assistant to simplify this
common task.

To find a specific address:

1. **Press and hold the Home button.**

   Siri will be ready for your instructions after the short
   chime.

2. **Tell Siri where you want to go by starting with "Take
   me to" or "Give me directions to," followed by the
   street address, city, and state.**

   You could, for example, say, "Take me to 1 Infinite
   Loop, Cupertino, California." (I bet you already
   knew that this address is in fact Apple's world
   headquarters.)

   Figures 3-1 and 3-2 show you what Siri comes up with.

   As you can see, Siri opens up the Maps application,
   powered by Google, and drops colored pushpins at
   your location and the final destination.

3. **Tap Start in the upper-right corner to begin the turn-
   by-turn directions.**

Figure 3-1: Siri confirms the address you want, before opening up the Maps app.

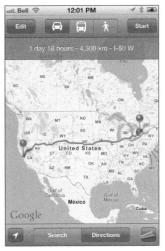

Figure 3-2: I'm pretty far away, but Siri's directions span the entire U.S.

In case you're not too familiar with Maps on the iPhone 4S (powered by Google), you can tap to select directions by car, public transit, or on foot, for more accurate directions based on your mode of travel. How are on-foot directions different from in-vehicle directions, you ask? You can walk any direction you like on a one-way street, cross through parks, and so on.

While you're on the way to your destination, you'll tap the right arrow (top right of the screen) to get the next written and visual directions. Figure 3-3 shows you what you'd see if you were traveling to California via Ann Arbor, Michigan.

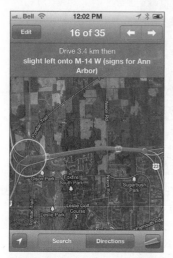

Figure 3-3: Here's what the map looks like while en route to your destination.

Because the Maps app on the iPhone 4S doesn't have voice-guided turn-by-turn directions, refrain from glancing down at the phone while behind the wheel. Hopefully, future versions of Siri will support audio-based directions so you can use it while driving.

Using Siri to find a location without an address

Siri isn't just for finding addresses you know; you can also ask Siri to take you to landmarks, attractions, and businesses.

For example, say you're in Orange County, California, and want to know how to get to Disneyland from there. You don't need to search for a specific address to the theme park in Anaheim — just let Siri know that you really want to see Mickey.

Like this:

1. **Press and hold the Home button.**

2. **Begin speaking after the short chime.**

   Tell Siri, "Take me to Disneyland!" (as if you've just won the Super Bowl).

   Siri opens up the Maps application, figures out where you are based on the iPhone 4S's GPS, and shows you the way to Disneyland.

3. **Pack up the kids and head out the door.**

   You'll see visual directions to the park, either with a standard view (see Figure 3-4), satellite view, or hybrid of the two (shown in Figure 3-5). Tap the small Page Turn icon in the lower-right corner of the Maps screen to make your selection.

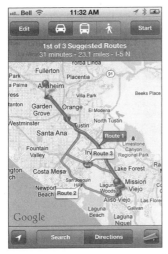

Figure 3-4: Siri will open Maps and show you the standard view to your destination.

Notice that the Maps app can show you alternate routes, where applicable, as you'll see here in Figure 3-6. In fact, the Maps app can often show you traffic information as well, if you like — just tap the lower right-hand corner of the screen and select "Show Traffic" (if available). This might sway you to take one route over another. Traffic near L.A.? Unheard of (cough)!

Figure 3-5: Alternatively, you can view the map using a satellite or hybrid view (the latter of which is shown here).

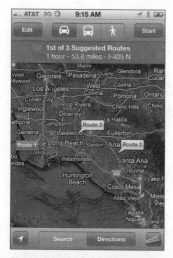

Figure 3-6: In this scenario, you can choose from one of three routes.

Asking Siri to see an address

One feature that many iPhone 4S users might not be aware of is the ability to *see* an address you want to travel to. Sticking with the Apple Inc. headquarters as an example, you can ask Siri to show you what the campus looks like and you'll see it on your screen within seconds.

After all, you might want to get an idea of the size of the place and what's around there and request the Street View of the area (if supported), which folds in real photos of the area! More on this in a moment.

To see what a location looks like:

1. **Press and hold the Home button.**

   The little chime you hear means Siri is listening for your instructions.

2. **Tell Siri about an address you'd like to see on the Maps application.**

   For example, say, "Siri, show me 1 Infinite Loop, Cupertino, California."

   Siri does what you ask. (Hey, she's your loyal personal assistant, after all.)

   The first view you'll see is of a standard top-down map view of the area, with 1 Infinite Loop front and center (see the pushpin in Figure 3-7).

3. **If you'd like, tap the screen to open up the Maps application, then tap the small Page Turn icon in the lower right-hand corner of the Maps screen to choose another view.**

   The hybrid view, which folds in satellite imagery, is kind of neat. (See Figure 3-8.)

One of my favorite features in Maps is the ability to jump down to Street View, if it's supported in that particular city and neighborhood. Tap the little orange icon of a person (refer to Figure 3-8) and you can then see the area as if you were standing on the street! (See Figure 3-9.) Use your fingertips to spin around 360 degrees or tap one of the arrows to "drive" down the street a few feet at a time, as in Figure 3-10. Neat, huh?

Be aware these photos might've been taken a few years ago — just in case you're looking for that neon Thai restaurant sign shown in Maps as a landmark, even though the joint went out of business in 2009.

Figure 3-7: Here's what Apple's campus looks like in standard Map view.

Figure 3-8: Tap the screen to open up the Maps app, allowing for more options.

Telling Siri to take you home

Had enough of where you are? Can't seem to figure out where you are? Realize you need to run home because you forgot to walk the dog? You can instruct Siri to take you home, wherever you are. It's as easy as asking.

Figure 3-9: Here's Apple's official headquarters, thanks to Google Maps with Street View.

Figure 3-10: Another look at Apple's main offices, using Street View.

You might need to tell Siri where "home" is if prompted to do so, but you'll need to do this only once.

1. **Press and hold the Home button.**

2. **After you hear the chime, simply tell Siri, "Take me home" or "How do I get home?"**

3. **Review what Siri is showing you.**

   Siri opens up your Maps app and drops a pushpin on your home address.

4. **Tap the right arrow on the top right of the screen and follow the written and visual instructions for going home. (See Figure 3-11.)**

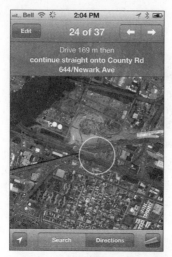

Figure 3-11: Even if you're in another state, you can get the fastest route home, thanks to Siri and the Maps app.

While you can tell Siri to take you home, you might not want to take advantage of this feature — especially if you don't make it a habit of locking your iPhone 4S. Why, you ask? If you lose your smartphone, a tech-savvy thief can ask Siri to "take me home" and know exactly where you live. Instead, perhaps you want to put your local shopping mall as your home address, as you can likely find your way home from there without any assistance. Just food for thought!

Telling Siri to direct you to someone in your Contacts list

Did you know that you can also ask Siri to take you to a friend or colleague's residence or workplace? You can say, "Take me to Mary Smith's house" or "Show me the way to mom's work." As long as you have the address of the person you're looking for in your Contacts app on the iPhone 4S, Siri can help out.

Here's an example:

1. **Press and hold the Home button.**

2. **After you hear the chime, simply tell Siri to take you to someone in your Contacts list.**

   For example, say, "Take me to Tore Dietrich's office." (See Figure 3-12.)

   Siri will find the contact in your address book, find the specific address you requested, and open your Maps app to show you the address, as shown in Figure 3-13.

3. **When you're ready to go, tap the right-pointing arrow and start your journey.**

4. **Follow the directions to get to your destination.**

Figure 3-12: Tell Siri to take you to someone's address in your address book — work or home.

Figure 3-13: Siri opens Google Maps and gives you directions.

Using Siri for Location-based Searches

Now let's take a look at how Siri can help you find establishments around your hometown — or even in another city.

For example, you can find a restaurant not just by name but also by type of food you're looking for. You can ask Siri to find a good place to eat based on what you're in the mood for. You'll see relevant restaurants listed by type of cuisine, proximity, and rating (thanks to the awesome Yelp service).

Here's an example of what you can do. And keep in mind that this is a great way to show off the power of Siri to friends, family, and colleagues!

1. **Press and hold the Home button.**

   You'll hear the familiar Siri chime, which means you can ask her to find a restaurant.

2. **Instruct Siri where you to want to go or what type of food you feel like eating.**

For example, tell Siri something like, "Find a good steak house near me," "Show me the best Italian food in New York," or "I'm in the mood for Indian cuisine." (See Figure 3-14 for an example.)

Siri shows you relevant results within a couple of seconds, as shown in Figure 3-15.

3. **Peruse the listings and tap the one that interests you the most.**

   After you tap a desired restaurant, Siri opens up the Maps application to show you where it is. You'll see the name of the restaurant clearly on the map; tap it for more detail, such as the exact address or phone number. Or, if you like, choose to add the address to Contacts or to Map Bookmarks, or get directions to the place from where you are.

Figure 3-14: I asked Siri for good Japanese food, so she sorted the results for me.

Remember, you can ask for a food or drink category (for example, "Find coffee near me") or be more specific ("Where is Starbucks?"). You can also ask Siri to search in different ways; Siri is amazingly versatile, so you can use language that's comfortable to you. You can even try slang like, "Show me the best burger joints in Atlanta." See Figure 3-16 for a slightly different approach.

Figure 3-15: Flick up on the results to see additional pages. Tap an entry for info and directions (if need be).

Figure 3-16: Siri lists many Mexican restaurants near me, all displayed by Yelp rating.

Siri's navigation and local business searches aren't available yet in Canada — at the time of writing this. Apple hasn't committed to a date, but many iPhone 4S users in the Great White North are hoping for support sooner than later. However, you can get directions to most anywhere if the destination address is in the U.S. (See Figure 3-17.)

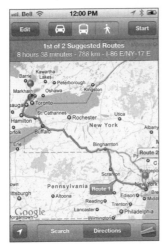

Figure 3-17: While you're using your iPhone 4S in Toronto, Canada, Siri can give directions to a U.S.-based address.

Siri's local searches aren't limited to only restaurants — but it's a fun place to start.

The following are a few other things you can ask or tell Siri, and you'll get a list of options, with navigation support:

✔ **"Find the nearest gas station."**

Driving on fumes? You can see a list of nearby stations to fill up your vehicle with fuel.

✔ **"Where is an ATM machine that's within walking distance?"**

Get turn-by-turn, on-foot directions to the closest bank machine.

✔ **"Siri, I feel sick."**

Your personal assistant shows you nearby clinics or hospitals.

✔ **"List the closest churches to me."**

Need to get a quick prayer in? If you like, be more specific (for example, include the words, "Catholic church" or ask for a "mosque" or "synagogue".)

✔ **"What's playing at the movies?"**

Siri brings up movie listings at nearby theaters.

See Figures 3-18, 3-19, and 3-20 for examples of location-based searches.

Figure 3-18: Don't run out of gas! Just ask Siri where to fill up.

Figure 3-19: Traveling to a city? Siri can scope out what you want before you get there.

Figure 3-20: Ask Siri to list medical clinics, and she'll comply. Or say you're not feeling well.

What's the Weather Like? Ask Siri!

The final section in this chapter covers all the ways Siri can fill you in on the weather — not just today but in the near future, too. And not just in your local area but in another city altogether!

A simple question to Siri can yield the answers you seek. But of course, that doesn't mean that the answers will always be accurate (neither is your favorite TV weatherperson).

As long as you have your iPhone 4S handy and a voice to ask Siri a few questions, you can get a quickie weather forecast right on the spot.

Here's an example of the most basic way Siri can help with your weather forecasting.

1. **Press and hold the Home button.**

    You'll hear the familiar Siri chime, which means you can begin talking.

2. **Ask Siri what the weather's like.**

   See Figure 3-21 for an example of what you can ask and how Siri responds. (Notice you also get a weeklong forecast!)

   Siri shows you the current weather for your city within a couple of seconds.

   Because the iPhone 4S is location-aware (thanks to its GPS chip), you don't need to tell Siri what city you're in.

Because Siri is context-sensitive, you can ask for the weather in different ways — and you'll likely get the response you seek. You might ask if it's cold outside. Or ask Siri to tell you the temperature. See Figure 3-22 for yet another way to phrase it.

Okay, so say you want to know what the weather's like in another city — perhaps you're planning a trip there — and it's still a few days away? No worries, as Siri can give you the local weather forecast and weather for multiple places around the globe (up to five days in the future).

For example, you may want to ask Siri what the weather is supposed to be like in London, England, on this coming Saturday. Figure 3-23 shows you how Siri would respond to that question.

Figure 3-21: Here, Siri responds when asked what it's like outside.

Figure 3-22: Ask and ye shall receive! Ask Siri if you need an umbrella (or say, "raincoat" and you might get a "yes").

Figure 3-23: Too bad the forecast isn't too promising for this weekend in London. Notice how Saturday's temperature is in blue font?

Here are some other examples of what you can ask Siri, when it comes to the weather:

- ✔ "How's the weather in Minneapolis right now?"
- ✔ "How hot will it be in Bangkok this weekend?"
- ✔ "What's the projected high for Montreal tomorrow?"
- ✔ "What's the forecast for tonight?"
- ✔ "Check the forecast for Washington, D.C., this week."
- ✔ "How windy is it outside?"
- ✔ "When is the sunrise tomorrow in Acapulco?
- ✔ "Will it rain in Dallas this week?"
- ✔ "Do I need a jacket tonight?"(See Figure 3-24)

Figure 3-24: How did we ever live before Siri? Here, she shows tonight's forecast.

Chapter 4

Using Siri for E-mail, Texting, and Phone Calls

*I*n this chapter — and it's one of the longer ones — you get to see how you can use Siri as your personal communication tool.

Specifically, your voice-activated personal assistant can be very handy for composing and accessing e-mails, composing and reading text messages (SMS), and placing a phone call to a particular number or someone in your Contacts (address book).

There's quite a lot to cover, so let's jump right in and begin.

"Siri, Take a Letter"

One of the most impressive — and convenient — things Siri can do is send your e-mails for you.

Siri can transcribe your words into text so that you only need to talk into your iPhone 4S. Siri will then type out the words you say, including the name of the person or group you're sending it to, the subject line, and the body of the message.

You'll find this can really speed up your "written" communication on your iPhone 4S. In fact, experts say talking is three to four times faster than typing. Plus, not everyone is as fast or accurate on an all-touch smartphone as they are on those button-based ones out there. (Think BlackBerry smartphones.)

In other words, using Siri for sending e-mails not only catches up to other phones, but blows past it.

In this chapter, I show you how to use Siri to send e-mails to family, friends, and colleagues — whether they're in your Contacts or not.

Although using Siri to type e-mails for you is incredibly convenient, resist doing it while you're behind the wheel of a moving vehicle. You still may need to glance at your phone to catch small errors — or at the very least you might be preoccupied with your e-mail instead of concentrating on driving — so be sure to send your messages after you've parked the car. After all, Siri can't call 9-1-1 for you.

Composing, Sending, and Accessing E-mails

You have two ways to start composing an e-mail using Siri. You can start right from your home screen — as if you just turned on your smartphone — by pressing and holding the Home button (or if it's set up to do so, by holding your iPhone up to your ear). The other way to have Siri transcribe your words into text is to start a message to someone the old fashioned way (typing), and then tap the microphone icon to start talking. Figure 4-1 shows you what you might see if you were to talk into your phone.

Here's a closer look at both options.

Figure 4-1: Siri types your spoken e-mails for you.

Starting and sending an e-mail from scratch

Okay, so you realize you need to send an e-mail to someone while you're walking down the street and you don't want to stop to type the message. There is a better way. Pull out your smartphone, press the Home button, and then start talking.

Here's the blow-by-blow account:

1. **Press and hold the Home button.**

   The little chime you hear means Siri is listening for your instructions.

2. **Say the word "E-mail" and then the name of the person you want to e-mail.**

   Siri opens your mail program and puts the name of the person you're e-mailing in the To field — if they're in your address book. (See the "E-mailing someone who isn't in your Contacts" section, later in this chapter, to find out how to e-mail someone who isn't in your Contacts.)

3. Dictate your e-mail.

When you're done, Siri shows you the contents of your message on the screen, as shown in Figure 4-2. For example, you can say "E-mail Mary Smith [short pause]. Hi Mary, hope you're having a good day. This is just a reminder about our meeting at 3 p.m. See you then."

Take advantage of the fact that Siri previews your e-mail by showing you the contents of your message on the screen by taking the time to review your e-mail, just in case you need to tweak it, add more recipients, and so on, before you send it.

Figure 4-2: Siri lets you review your e-mail before sending it.

Siri next asks you, "What's the subject of your e-mail?"

4. Say what you'd like the subject line to say, such as, "Meeting confirmation."

Siri again shows you what your e-mail currently looks like — now you should be able to see the person you're sending it to, what the subject is, and the body of the e-mail. Siri says, "Here's what your e-mail looks like. Ready to send it?" If you're in fact ready to send it, you can let 'er fly.

5. Review all fields, and then say, "Okay," "Yes," "No," or "Cancel."

Alternatively, you can tap the appropriate response — Cancel or Send— if you prefer.

If you say "Yes" or tap Send, then it's bye-bye e-mail. Your e-mail message is sent, and you'll hear that iPhone "whoosh" sound as a confirmation.

If you say "No" or tap Cancel, the message is canceled, and you'll see a large red CANCELED stamp across the message. It won't be saved as a draft.

 It might take you a bit to get the hang of composing and sending e-mails with Siri. When you're starting an e-mail, remember that you can do these things:

- ✔ **Teach Siri who your contacts are.** When you're starting an e-mail and say, "E-mail Dad," for the first time, Siri asks who your dad is. You're prompted to tap the contact name in your Contacts listing for your dad. Going forward, you can simply say, "E-mail Dad," and Siri knows whose address to retrieve; you won't have to tap the name again.

- ✔ **Correct mistakes and make other changes.** If you make a mistake and need to change your e-mail, say, "Change subject," or "Change e-mail," and then give Siri a revised message for the recipient. In Figure 4-3, for example, Siri misspelled my name (Mark instead of Marc, believe it or not), but it allowed me to correct the mistake by repeating the request a few times and Siri, the third time, finally showed me "Marc" instead of "Mark," and so I accepted.

- ✔ **Tell Siri which e-mail address to send a message to.** If you have multiple e-mail addresses for someone in your Contacts, you can instruct Siri to e-mail a specific address. For example, you might have a friend with a work and home e-mail address, and don't want to send a private message about an upcoming party to your best friend's work address. Simply tell Siri "E-mail [friend's name]," followed by "[work or home]," followed by "[message]." Also, if you have more than one, say, Mary Smith in your Contacts, it might ask you to select one over another.

- ✔ **Cancel messages.** To cancel the message altogether, say "No" or "Cancel" when Siri asks you if it's OK to send the message. Alternatively, remember you can always tap the microphone button to cancel your last request. If you want to make sure that Siri understood you, check to see if a large red CANCELED stamp appears across your e-mail message, as shown in Figure 4-4.

Figure 4-3: Siri allows you to edit messages.

Figure 4-4: A large CANCELED stamp appears across any message you choose not to send.

✔ **Have Siri type the subject line first.** To do so, say "subject" right after you say the receiver's name, and Siri regards the next few words out of your mouth as the subject line, as shown in Figure 4-5. Only after she enters the subject does she prompt you to dictate the body of the e-mail.

For example, say "E-Mail Mary Smith [slight pause], work, subject [slight pause], meeting confirmation." Now, press the Home button or wait a second, and Siri will ask you, "Okay, what would you like the e-mail to say?" Now you can dictate the body of the e-mail and have Siri send it for you, hands-free.

Figure 4-5: Say the e-mail subject line first and then dictate the body.

Having Siri finish an e-mail you started to type

The second way you can send an e-mail through Siri is to start an e-mail the regular way — by tapping the E-mail icon and then tapping to select to whom you're sending the message. The screen shown in Figure 4-6 appears. Notice the microphone icon at the bottom of the screen, to the left of the space bar. Simply tap that icon and begin speaking into the iPhone 4S; you'll see your words appear on the white canvas, as if you were typing them yourself. Before you send it, however, quickly scan for errors in case Siri misunderstood a couple of your words.

Did you know you can also fold the subject into your e-mail message at the same time you ask Siri to start it for you? For example, you can say, "E-mail my wife about the vacation," and Siri will start a message for you to your wife (because you've already told Siri who she is) and the word "vacation" will be in the subject line. Next, Siri will ask you, "What do you want the e-mail to say?" Better yet, you can say something like, "E-mail Mom and Dad about the luncheon and say I had a great time," and Siri will populate all the fields of the e-mail message for you!

Figure 4-6: Tap the microphone icon to dictate your e-mail inside the message.

If you're really ambitious, you can have Siri create an e-mail for you, populate the To field, give a subject, and type the message for you — all in one breath. In other words, you can tell Siri where to send the e-mail, the subject line, and the body of the e-mail all at once. Not many people know this trick! As you'll see in Figure 4-7, I gave Siri all of this info at the same time: "E-mail Mike Jones about the article and say Hi Mike, I think this should work." Talk about a time saver, huh?

Sending e-mail to groups

You can have Siri send an e-mail to a number of people at once — and you won't believe how easy it is. Just follow these steps:

1. **Say everyone's name you want to e-mail the message to.**

Figure 4-7: Siri lets you say all three parts to the e-mail, all in one shot.

For instance, say, "Send an e-mail to Dad and my wife and Mary Smith and Mike Jones."

Note that you must say "and" in between each of the recipient's names. If Siri is unsure about someone (such as having three contacts with the name Kellie or Kelly), Siri will ask you to confirm which one you want to send the correspondence to.

Siri asks, "What would you like to say to these four people?" and you'll see them all in the To field, as shown in Figure 4-8.

2. **Answer Siri by dictating your group message.**

   Siri asks if you're ready to send it.

3. **Say "Yes" to send the message.**

   You'll hear the iPhone confirmation sound, confirming that the message was sent.

4. **(Optional) If you need to tweak a couple of things, tap anywhere on the screen and make your changes before sending.**

   Note that, if you decide to manually tweak your message, the e-mail now looks like one you may have typed from the get-go. (See Figure 4-9.)

Figure 4-8: A message to a group looks just like a message to a single recipient.

Figure 4-9: Tap anywhere on the screen to make changes.

Siri e-mail grab bag

Siri is multitalented, so you might have trouble keeping up with all she can do. The following list gives you an idea of the range of things Siri can do:

✔ **Sending an e-mail while wearing a headset, microphone, or Bluetooth headset.** If you're using headphones with a remote and microphone on the cord, simply press and hold the center button to talk to Siri. If you're wearing a Bluetooth headset, on the other hand, press and hold the call button to bring up Siri's tone, which means you can begin asking a question or giving a command. Keep in mind, however, that speakerphones in your vehicle might not work as well with Siri, since your mouth is farther away from the microphone, which can pick up more background noise.

✔ **Including punctuation in an e-mail message.** To do so, just say it out loud. For example, to finish a sentence you can say, "period." Asking a question? Then be sure to say, "question mark," at the end of the sentence. You can also say, "exclamation mark," "comma," "semicolon," "quote" (or "quotation mark"), and so on.

You can even say, "smiley face," and you'll see the emoticon (sideways smiley face) on the screen! See Figure 4-10 for an example of Siri's work — with 100 percent accuracy, no less.

✔ **If you're unsure what Siri can do, just ask!** You can literally ask your personal assistant what she (a female voice in North America) is capable of, and you'll see a laundry list of things she can perform for you. If you want specific examples, tap one of Siri's initial suggestions. For instance, if you want to know how to use Siri for sending e-mails, tap the line that says "E-mail Lisa about the trip," and this will open up a dozen more examples of ways to use Siri for e-mail.

Figure 4-10: Testing the punctuation options, including "exclamation mark" and "smiley face"!

CCing and BCCing contacts in an e-mail

Just like in a regular e-mail, you can send an e-mail to one person and carbon copy, or CC, another person, so they also receive the same e-mail as the main recipient.

As you'd expect with Siri, all you need to do is send an e-mail to someone (in my example from Figure 4-11, that person is Mary Smith) and then take a short pause, say "CC," then mention someone else from your Contacts (in this case, Mike Jones). Then you can say "subject" and tell Siri what you want your subject line to be.

Alternatively, you can say "carbon copy" instead of "CC." Figure 4-12 shows this method works, too.

And of course, you can also "BCC" or *blind carbon copy* someone when sending an e-mail. For the uninitiated, speci-fying "BCC" means someone else *is* included on the e-mail — but the main recipient won't have a clue because he or she won't see any mention of the other person's name or e-mail address.

Figure 4-11: Saying "CC" keeps someone else in the loop.

Figure 4-12: Saying "carbon copy" works as well.

It's considered proper *netiquette* (Internet etiquette) not to blitz a number of people at once and reveal all of their e-mail addresses to everyone. To respect people's privacy, it's better to BCC people instead. Doing it with Siri is simple: Just say, "BCC," or "blind carbon copy," and say the person(s) e-mail address you want to hide and you'll see that person's name appear in the BCC area of your e-mail message. For an example of this technique, check out Figure 4-13.

Of course, you can CC one person (or many people) and BCC someone else (or a whole bunch of somebody elses) within the same e-mail.

Figure 4-13: Add e-mail recipients to the blind carbon copy field of the message by simply saying "BCC."

More E-mail Tasks Siri Can Do for You

As late-night infomercial guru Ron Popeil says, "But wait; there's more!" Siri can also do these e-mail–related tasks for you.

E-mailing someone who isn't in your Contacts

In earlier sections of this chapter, I discuss e-mailing people who are already in your Contacts. But what if you need to send an e-mail to someone who's not listed there?

Using Siri to send an e-mail to a specific address — one you might not have in your Contacts or care to add — is as simple as speaking the address aloud.

Here's how to do it:

1. **Press and hold the Home button and tell Siri to send an e-mail to someone by saying their complete e-mail address.**

   For example, to send an e-mail to `richard.anderson@ bigtimeisp.com` (just making this one up), simply say, "E-mail Richard dot Anderson at bigtimeisp dot com."

   You'll see the e-mail address appear in the To field, as shown in Figure 4-14.

2. **Add a subject and dictate your e-mail.**

   Siri transcribes your words, and then asks if you're ready to send the e-mail.

3. **(Optional) If you need to tweak a couple of things, tap anywhere on the screen and make your changes before sending.**

4. **Say, "Yes," to send the message.**

   You'll hear the iPhone confirmation sound to confirm the message was sent.

   Siri won't add this person to your Contacts.

Figure 4-14: Asking Siri to enter an e-mail address.

Finding e-mails in your inbox

Guess what? Siri isn't only good for transcribing your voice into e-mail messages. Siri can also help you find e-mails.

✔ **Most recent messages:** For example, say you have a few hundred messages in your inbox but you want to find the most recent ones? You can simply tell Siri, "Check e-mail" and you'll immediately see the last 25 e-mail messages that arrived in your inbox.

✔ **From a specific person:** You can ask, "Any new e-mail from Matt today?" and Siri will show you any e-mails received today from anyone named Matt. Or you can say, "Show the e-mail from Lisa yesterday." Figure 4-15 shows the kinds of things such a request might pull up.

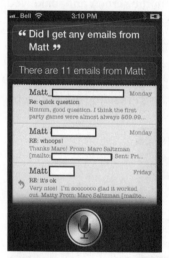

Figure 4-15: Here, I asked Siri if I'd received any e-mails from "Matt."

✔ **Based on the subject line:** You can tell Siri, "Show new e-mail about the doctor's appointment," or "Show e-mail about the rent," and Siri will pull up any relevant messages for you.

Replying to and forwarding messages

Siri won't just send an e-mail for you. It's also possible to reply to or forward an e-mail you've already received. For example, while you're reading an e-mail you can hold down the Home button and tell Siri, "Reply Dear Julie, sorry I had to cancel plans for Saturday's lunch. I'll call you later to chat about another date."

To forward a message, press and hold the Home button while inside of the e-mail and say something like, "Forward e-mail to Phil." Siri will ask you if you want to add a message as well ("What do you want the e-mail to say?"). See Figure 4-16 for an example of me forwarding a note to my wife, Kellie.

Figure 4-16: In this example, I told Siri to forward this e-mail message to my wife, Kellie.

Composing, Replying to, and Reading Text Messages

Siri is great when it comes to composing, sending, forwarding, and accessing all your e-mails on your iPhone 4S, but don't for a second think that Siri can deal with only e-mail. If you're of an age to think e-mail is old school and that texting is the wave of the future, that won't throw Siri for a loop. She can text with the best of them.

You might already be using the iMessage app bundled on your smartphone — who can resist such a quick, reliable, and inexpensive way to communicate with friends and family between phones (regardless of the model?) — but Siri makes it even more handy. And frankly, texting is now a lot more fun, too.

Not only can you use Siri to dictate text messages for you, just as you do for e-mail, but Siri can also read your unread text messages aloud, too! (Nope, Siri can't do this for e-mails but she *can* for texts.) Now you can continue your jog down the beach without pulling out your smartphone and you can ask Siri to read your texts out loud to you. How convenient, eh?

This portion of the chapter outlines how texting with Siri works, including what you need to say for it to work smoothly, and what you'll hear back as a response.

Composing a text message

Sending a text message with your voice is incredibly fast and accurate.

There are a couple of different ways to text using Siri. If you'd like to do it one step at a time, the following is the most basic way to compose a text message:

1. **Press and hold the Home button.**

   Wait for the short chime and begin speaking.

2. **Say the word "Text" and then the name of the person you want to send a text message to.**

Siri opens your iMessage app and puts the name of the person you're texting in the To field — if he or she is in your Contacts, that is. Flip forward a few pages to see how to text someone who isn't in your Contacts.

3. **In response to Siri's prompt ("What do you want your message to say?"), dictate your text message.**

   When you're done, Siri shows you the message and asks you if you want to send it.

4. **Say "Yes" or "Send" to send the message. Or say "No" or "Cancel" to cancel the message.**

   If it's sent, you'll hear the standard whoosh confirmation sound, and the message disappears. (To see it, open up your iMessage app and see the conversation tree with that particular person; your sent texts will be in green.) Figure 4-17 shows what a typical text message would like look, as transcribed by Siri.

Figure 4-17: Texting is as easy as saying, "Text," followed by the name of the person you want to send the message to.

If you choose not to send a text message you've composed, Siri will ask you what you'd like to do with the message, as shown in Figure 4-18. At the top of the screen, you'll see, "To continue, you can Send, Cancel, Review, or Change it." As you'd expect, saying "Send" sends the text; "Cancel" cancels the message; "Review" reads it to you; and "Change" lets you tweak using the keyboard, if need be.

Figure 4-18: As you'll see here, you're given options if you tell Siri not to send the message.

You don't always have to say the word "Text" to tell Siri you want to start a text message. You can also say something like, "Message," or "Tell," followed by the person or phone number you want to send the text message to! Try it; you'll like it.

Another way to compose a text message is to say the person's name you want to text and the message — all in one breath, without waiting for Siri's prompt. Since texts are usually shorter than e-mails, you might opt to do this to save time. Don't worry; Siri can handle this without a hitch.

An example of what this might look like follows:

1. **Press and hold the Home button.**

   Begin talking after the chime.

2. **Tell Siri, "Text" and the person's name; after a very short pause, say the message aloud, too.**

   You'll hear a high ping, which means Siri is processing your command, and then you'll see your text message.

3. **Review the text message and, if it looks good to you, say "Send" or "Yes." (If it doesn't look good, say "No" or "Cancel" to cancel the message.)**

Siri will do what you ask, of course. That's her job as your faithful personal assistant. Figure 4-19 shows an example of a canceled message.

Figure 4-19: Just like a canceled e-mail, Siri stamps the word CANCELED in red.

If you have a few different phone numbers for someone in your address book, you might find it easier to specify what number to send the text message to right away. For example, tell Siri, "Message Susan on her mobile that I'll be late for our 2 p.m. coffee." Saying "on her mobile" eliminates any doubt Siri might have about what number to send the text to.

Texting more than one person

Just as you can send an e-mail to multiple people through Siri, it's also possible to compose and send a text message to more than one recipient. (For sending group e-mails, see earlier in this chapter on how to pull that off via Siri.)

In fact, this can really help save you time. All you need to do is ask Siri to send the text to multiple people, like this:

1. **Press and hold the Home button.**

   You'll hear a short chime, which means Siri is ready for you.

2. **Tell Siri "Text" the name of the first person you'd like to text, "and," and the name of the second person.**

   It's important you say the word "and" between all the names!

   You can add as many people as you like. You can also wait for Siri to respond with, "What would you like the message to say?" or start saying the message after you tell Siri to whom you're sending the message (a short pause is best). Figure 4-20 shows what a request for a text message to multiple recipients looks like.

Figure 4-20: Siri transcribes your instructions and shows it to you before opening up the iMessage app (see Figure 4-21). You don't need to say or touch anything to go to the text view in the next screen capture.

3. **Review the text message (see Figure 4-21) and, if you like what you see, say "Yes" or "Send." If not, say "No" or "Cancel" and you'll be prompted with other options, as shown back in Figure 4-18.**

   If you opt for "Yes" or "Send," Siri sends the same text message to multiple recipients.

Figure 4-21: Here's what the text message to multiple people looks like.

As you can see in Figure 4-21, you sometimes won't be able to see all the recipients Siri will send the text message to. If this concerns you — for fear of sending the text to the wrong person — you can tap the screen, which opens up the text message within iMessage, and you'll see all additional recipients listed clearly here.

If punctuation is important to you, remember to say things like "comma," "period," and "question mark" inside your text message.

Composing a text message from within iMessage

Just like e-mailing on your iPhone 4S, you can start a text message the old-fashioned way — by opening up iMessage and selecting to whom the note will be sent — but then finish it off with your voice, if you like.

Perhaps you decide it would be faster to dictate your text message instead of typing it out. You don't need to close down the message and start again.

Here's what you do:

1. **In iMessage, tap the icon of a little microphone, just to the left of the space bar. (See Figure 4-22.)**

2. **Speak your text message clearly, then tap the word Done when you're finished.**

   Siri shows your words on the screen.

3. **If what you see onscreen is accurate — the words are what you said — then tap the green Send button to the right of the speech window.**

   Siri sends your text message.

Figure 4-22: See that little microphone icon? Tap it to begin speaking.

Hearing Your Text Messages Read Aloud

Ah, this is one of the coolest features of Siri: the option to hear your texts read out loud to you.

Say you've got a bunch of unread text messages on your iPhone and you don't want to tap through each one. After all, you might be concentrating on something you're looking at — er, like the road in front of your vehicle.

Siri can read your text messages to you in a human-like voice, and you can even respond to them using your voice, too. Now that's hands-free.

Here's how to have Siri read your text messages out loud:

1. **Press and hold the Home button.**

   After the short chime, you can give Siri a command.

2. **Say something like, "Read me my texts."** See Figure 4-23.

   You can make the same request a number of different ways. "Do I have any messages?" works just great.

   Siri announces how many messages you have waiting for you. Siri then starts reading all new messages to you, beginning with the sender's name — or if the name is unknown, the phone number it's coming from. You won't see the message on the screen.

Figure 4-23: While you don't see the words here, Siri is reading my new texts to me aloud.

3. **When prompted by Siri to say what you want to do with the message, say either "Reply" or "Read them again."**

Siri performs the action requested. See Figure 4-24 for an example of my reply to my wife Kellie's text message.

Figure 4-24: Say "Reply" and dictate your reply to the sender. Siri sends the message when you're done.

Keep in mind that Siri will read only those text messages that you haven't picked up yet. If you've got a bunch of messages stored on your phone but you've already read and/or replied to them, Siri will tell you there isn't anything to read to you. Figure 4-25 shows you what you'd hear and see on your iPhone 4S screen in such a situation.

You have a number of options when it comes to responding to a text message. The following are a few commands that Siri can handle:

- ✔ **"Reply that's a great idea, thanks."**
- ✔ **"Reply saying that's a great idea, thanks."**
- ✔ **"Tell her I'll be there in 15 minutes."**
- ✔ **"Call him."**
- ✔ **"E-mail her."**
- ✔ **"Read it again."**

Figure 4-25: Siri tells me there are no new messages because she speaks the text of only unread messages.

Sending a Text Message to a Phone Number

Okay, so say you're given a phone number to text, but it isn't stored in your Contacts. No problem, as Siri can be used to send a text to a 10-digit number, if you prefer.

Maybe you don't want to add someone to your address book or it's a one-time text (such as a contest you need to enter via SMS).

All you need to do is say the phone number you want to text, and Siri will know what to do. For instance, do this:

1. **Press and hold the Home button.**

   Siri chimes, letting you know you can start talking.

2. **Tell Siri the phone number to text.**

   As an example, tell Siri, "Text 212-555-1212 [short pause] Enter me in the drawing, thanks."

   You can also say, "Message," or "Tell," instead of "Text."

Siri shows you the number you want to send the text message to as well as your message.

3. **After previewing the number and text message, say "Yes" or "Send," and Siri will do the rest. If you don't want to send the text, say "No" or "Cancel."**

See Figure 4-26 for an example of texting a number instead of the name of someone in your Contacts.

Figure 4-26: Sending a text to a phone number is as easy as saying a name.

Siri won't decipher acronyms or text-speak, so if someone sends you a message with "LOL" or "TTYL," Siri won't say "laugh out loud" or "talk to you later," respectively.

Also be aware that you can't send a picture or video message via Siri. If you said, "Text a photo to my wife," it won't ask you which photo to attach; instead Siri will think you want to text the words "a photo" to your wife.

Calling a Number or Person (and Starting FaceTime Chats, Too!)

The final part of this chapter covers how you can use Siri to call someone in your Contacts or any phone number you want to call.

Okay, calling a phone number isn't the most ground-breaking thing Siri can do — cellphones have been able to "voice dial" for many years now — but you'll find Siri is a lot more accurate at the task. How many times have you said into an old phone "Call home" and your phone replies with "Calling Dr. Lome." Sigh.

As with all other Siri tasks, all you have to do is ask Siri to perform a task, and she will comply.

1. **Press and hold the Home button.**

2. **Wait for the short chime and then give Siri the command.**

   For example, you can say "Call" and give the person's name.

   As long as the person is in your Contacts, Siri will call the person for you.

 If you have multiple phone numbers for an individual, Siri might not know which phone number to use. That's why she may (politely) ask for a bit of clarification, as shown in Figure 4-27.

Figure 4-27: Tell Siri the person you want to call. Siri might ask to confirm which number to dial (work, home, and so on).

If you know that a contact listing has multiple phone numbers, you can go ahead and specify which number to dial, like this:

1. **Press and hold the Home button.**

2. **Begin talking after the short chime.**

   You could say "Call [person's name] mobile." Or "Call [person's name] home." Or "Call [person's name] work."

   You get the idea. Siri knows which number to call because you're more specific. (See Figures 4-28 and 4-29.)

Figure 4-28: Specify which telephone number Siri should dial.

 You can tell Siri who the important people are in your life — such as "husband," "mom," or "brother" — and Siri remembers. For instance, after you tell Siri your wife's name and Siri associates "wife" with the appropriate Contacts listing, you can tell Siri to "Call my wife on her work phone," and the task will be performed. You can also specify your home and office numbers for Siri; after doing that, you can say things like, "Call home."

If you want to call a phone number that's not in your Contacts, you can do it by saying the 10-digit number verbally:

1. **Press and hold the Home button.**

2. **Tell Siri what you'd like — but wait for the familiar chime first.**

   You can say "Call" and give the phone number. Or say "Dial" and give the phone number. (See Figure 4-30.)

   Siri dials the number for you right away, of course.

Figure 4-29: Siri dials the number you requested, such as "home," "office," or "mobile."

Figure 4-30: Siri can help dial a phone number to someone who isn't in your Contacts.

Finally, were you aware that Siri can even help make a FaceTime call to someone?

"What's FaceTime?" you ask. Apple's FaceTime is a free application built into many iOS devices (such as iPhone, iPod touch, and iPad 2) and Mac computers, allowing you to make video calls to friends, family, and colleagues — meaning they see you and you see them.

Think of FaceTime like its (probably more famous) competitor, Skype, but you can use FaceTime only over Wi-Fi (a wireless network) and not over a cellular connection. See Figures 4-31 and 4-32.

Imagine, then, that you have a friend in your Contacts and you'd like to FaceTime with them. Without Siri, you'd have to open up your Contacts, get to your friend's information, and tap the FaceTime button. Boring and time-consuming, right?

Figure 4-31: FaceTime on iPhone is more fun than a phone call because you can see to whom you're talking.

Figure 4-32: FaceTime can be done between multiple Apple products. Here are iPod touch devices.

With Siri, however, you only need to speak the instructions — no matter what you're doing on the iPhone at that time.

Here's the step-by-step process:

1. **Press and hold the Home button.**

   Wait for the tone.

2. **Tell Siri the name of the person you want to FaceTime with, like this: "FaceTime Maya."**

   See Figure 4-33 for an example of this.

   Siri begins calling Maya's FaceTime address on the spot — if Maya is in your Contacts — and you'll hear the phone ringing, as if you dialed it manually.

Figure 4-33: Tell Siri the person you'd like to FaceTime with, and the call is made.

Chapter 5

Getting the 4-1-1

- -

- -

*Y*our iPhone 4S is likely your lifeline to the world — and that includes finding information you seek, when and where you need it.

But searching for online information can be a time-consuming endeavor — especially if you need to open up the browser, tap the search box, type out a query, and wait for results (which you must then wade through).

A much easier way to get the information you need is to ask Siri to provide it for you. Using your voice, simply state your request, and you should receive an answer on the spot.

This goes for *everything* — from finding recipes to locating a country on a map, from accessing currency exchanges and movie listings to finding definitions of words, deciphering mathematical equations, and figuring out the current price of gas in your neighborhood.

This chapter is designed to help you unlock Siri's information-based abilities, which you'll likely come to rely upon more and more once you see what it can do for you. Really, this is pretty powerful stuff.

I cover how to use Siri quickly and efficiently, so you can speed up your search and get more accurate results. Of course, I'll pepper the chapter with examples of what you can ask and what you'll see and hear as a response.

If you're ready to master Siri's information pipeline, read on for the 4-1-1.

Getting Info

Apple has partnered with Wolfram | Alpha — one of the world's leading sources for expert knowledge and computation — to power Siri's on-demand information feature.

Whether you want to know what the *Family Guy* TV show is all about, who won the World Series in 1990, or need to figure out how much to tip the waitress at your local restaurant, the answers are just a quick question away.

If Wolfram | Alpha doesn't know the answer — and you'd be surprised at how much this database holds — Siri will suggest a web search, which I'll get to later in this chapter.

To see what hoops you can have Wolfram | Alpha jump through, start with some fact-based basic questions and answers.

Word definitions (and other fun stuff)

Imagine you have a question on the brain that's been bugging you and you want Siri to answer it. Maybe you came across a word in a book or heard it on the radio and have no clue what it means. Don't worry; it happens to the best of us.

Here's an example of how Siri, via Wolfram | Alpha, can help:

1. **Press and hold the Home button.**

2. **Listen for the chime and then ask your question.**

    Ask away. In Figure 5-1, you can see that I'm asking Siri to define a word.

    Siri shows you the definition and part of speech (such as noun, verb, or adjective) and, in many cases, Siri also shows you how to pronounce the word, the number of letters and syllables contained in the word, its first known use in English, its origins, its synonyms, its word frequency, its use in phrases, and more. (Figures 5-2 and 5-3 show the wealth of information Siri provides.)

Figure 5-1: Get the definition of a word on the fly with Siri and Wolfram|Alpha.

Figure 5-2: You get a lot more than just the definition of a word.

Figure 5-3: With many words, you even get crossword puzzle hints and Scrabble scores! Now that's detail.

If you ask Siri to define a word and it's not available in the Wolfram Alpha database or Siri can't quite make out your pronunciation, you're prompted to do a web search instead. But in the interest of time, try your word again and ensure you're saying it clearly — and be sure to minimize background noise. You might get the definition the second time around.

As you might've seen in other chapters in this book, you can ask Siri questions in different ways. To define a word, you can ask, "What does the word *photosynthesis* mean?" or "What's the definition of *photosynthesis*," or even "Define *photosynthesis*." See Figure 5-4 for an example of the latter.

Siri varies her response every time you ask, too, by saying things like, "Okay, here you go," "I found this for you," or "This might answer your question."

If you'd like a few more examples of the kinds of things Siri can help with, try one (or all) of the following:

✔ **"What's the circumference of Mars?"**

Answer: 13,260 miles (Actually, Siri knew I was in Canada, so I was first presented with 21,340 kilometers.)

- ✔ **"How long do dogs live?"**

  Answer: 15 to 20 years

- ✔ **"What was the Best Picture winner in 1970?"**

  Answer: *Midnight Cowboy*

- ✔ **"How many calories are in a piece of cake?"**

  Answer: Approximately 239 calories

- ✔ **"How many meters are in a foot?"**

  Answer: 0.3048 meters (or 12 inches)

- ✔ **"How deep is the Pacific ocean?"**

  Answer: About 14,108 feet

- ✔ **"What is the population of China?"**

  Answer: 1.35 billion people

- ✔ **"What is the highest mountain in the world?"**

  Answer: Mount Everest, at 8,850 meters

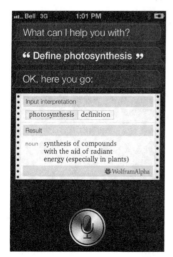

Figure 5-4: Cut out the small talk. You can ask Siri to define a word by saying "Define," followed by the word.

In Chapter 7, you'll take a look at all the weird, wacky, and wonderful things Siri can say to you or show you, but here's one question you might not think to ask: "What planes are overhead?" As you'd expect, Siri will tell you all the airliners above your head at that particular moment — including airline numbers — and show you a diagram, too. Check out Figures 5-5 and 5-6 for a quick look at what you might see.

Figure 5-5: Here is the first page of results you'll get when asking Wolfram|Alpha what planes are overhead.

Figure 5-6: You'll even get some visuals to complement the airlines, flight numbers, altitude, and angle.

Solving math problems

Siri and Wolfram I Alpha aren't one-trick ponies. While this powerful duo can help define words and answer some great trivia questions, they're also ideal for asking math-related questions.

For example, you're at your bank machine and you need to deposit a few checks. You have three main options: add the numbers up in your head or on paper, pull out a calculator (perhaps on your smartphone), or for the fastest solution, just ask Siri for the answer.

Here's what a typical exchange might look like:

1. **Press and hold the Home button.**

2. **Ask your question after you hear the familiar chime.**

   In this example, tell Siri the amounts of each check and ask for a total.

   Siri crunches the numbers for you and displays the answer on the screen, as shown in Figure 5-7.

3. **Double-check the amounts you gave — you'll see it on the screen, too — to ensure Siri heard you correctly,**

4. **If you're all good, press the Home button to close Wolfram I Alpha.**

Figure 5-7: Siri is awesome at helping you with math, such as adding up these four checks.

There are different ways to say numbers, including decimal points, if you need Siri to add it all up. For $220, for example, you can say "two-twenty" or "two-hundred and twenty." For $220.20, you can say "two-twenty point twenty," "two-twenty dot twenty," or "two-twenty dot two zero," and so on. Remember, Siri is amazingly versatile.

Siri isn't just limited to addition; you can also ask questions that involve subtraction, multiplication, and division — or a combination of them all. See Figure 5-8 for an example of this. *Note:* You can say "plus" or "add," "minus" or "take away," "multiply" or "times," and so on. Siri usually doesn't have a problem figuring out what you want.

Figure 5-8: Can you say homework helper? Kids, rejoice! Parents, cue the eye-rolling.

Or how about percentages and square roots? Fractions? No problem.

One of my favorite ways to use Siri — and wow my friends in the process — is when I'm trying to figure out how much to leave as a tip on a bill with multiple people.

The following is an example of what you can do.

1. Press and hold the Home button.

2. **Ask your math question after the short chime.**

   For this example, ask Siri something like, "What is an 18 percent tip on $490.10 for four people?"

   Within a second or two, Siri gives you the answer. (See Figure 5-9.)

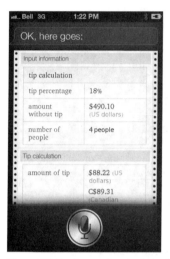

Figure 5-9: Don't get a headache trying to figure out a bill. Siri to the rescue!

3. **Scroll up on the results screen and you'll see additional information, as shown in Figure 5-10.**

4. **Close Siri, pay your $22 per person, and everyone goes home feeling like it was fair (except John, who didn't drink any wine, but that's another story).**

Stock quotes and more

You have a few fast ways to find out how your stocks are doing on the iPhone 4S. One solution is to drag your finger down from the top of the screen to open up the Notification Center. You can customize the real-time ticker you see here.

But using Siri is also a great way to see the information you seek. Plus, there's a lot more you can ask — as you'll see in a moment.

Figure 5-10: More info is given, if desired — including customary tip amounts, rounding up or down, and more.

Here's what you'd do if you want to ask the stock price for a particular company:

1. **Press and hold the Home button.**

2. **Ask your question after the short chime.**

   For example, you could ask, "Siri, how is Google doing today?" or "What is the Apple stock price at now?"

   Siri reads the info for you and displays it visually as well, all courtesy of Yahoo! Finance. (See Figure 5-11.)

3. **If you want to get more information, just tap the screen, which opens up the Stocks app for iPhone.**

   Here you'll see a lot more information about the company in question, the stock market as a whole, fluctuations over time, and more. See Figures 5-12, 5-13, and 5-14 for your options.

You can try to fool Siri, but it won't likely work. I asked what the Facebook stock price was at — knowing they haven't yet gone public, at least at the time of writing this — and I was advised by Siri there isn't a Facebook stock. LOL. I tried!

Figure 5-11: In this example, I asked Siri how Apple's stock was doing.

Figure 5-12: Tap the stock summary for more info courtesy of Yahoo! Finance.

Here are a few other stock-related questions you can ask Siri. Try it; you'll like it.

✓ "How are the markets doing?"

✓ "What did the NASDAQ close at today?"

✓ "What is the Nikkei Index at today?"

✓ "What is Yahoo's PE ratio?"

✓ "What did Microsoft close at today?"

Figure 5-13: More info.

Figure 5-14: Even more info.

Currency conversion

Uh-oh. You're on the phone with a hotel in Paris, France, and the desk clerk wants to know if you want the room for two hundred euros (€200) per night. Problem is, you have no idea how much that is in American dollars.

You can open up your web browser and try to find the answer while the Frenchman snobbishly sighs on the other end of the line, awaiting your prolonged reply. Or you can politely put him on hold for a moment, ask Siri for the answer, and tell him "yes" faster than he can say "*coq au vin.*"

Here's an example of how Siri can help with currency conversion:

1. **Press and hold the Home button.**

2. **Wait for the chime and begin speaking.**

   Sticking with my example scenario, you could ask Siri, "How much is 200 euros in American dollars?" Or you can ask for "U.S. dollars."

   Siri displays the answer for you visually, and even shows you exchange history and other currency exchange examples if you scroll up. (See Figures 5-15 and 5-16.)

Figure 5-15: Ask Siri to convert from one country's currency into another.

Figure 5-16: Flick your finger up to see additional exchanges.

You can even shorten your question to Siri. Because the iPhone 4S is location-aware, you can even ask, "How much is 200 euros?" and it'll automatically convert it to U.S. dollars for you. Or you can flip around the question by asking, "How many dollars is 200 euros?" If you're in Canada, it'll give you the conversion to Canadian funds, and so on.

Web Searching

Where would we be without the web? Not only do we have access to a world of information at our fingertips, but with Siri, you can get what you need even faster — and anywhere you've got your iPhone 4S handy.

As you see earlier in this chapter, Wolfram|Alpha has a ton of information ready for you, without having to search the web through Google or other search engines — from homework help to maps of the Heathrow airport. But there will be times you want to access the web for even more info while on the go. (Remember, even for Wolfram|Alpha you'll always need a data connection to use Siri.)

This portion of the chapter illustrates what you can search for, what kinds of results you can expect, and ways to optimize your results based on your verbal queries.

The first thing you might want to try is a basic web search about anything currently on your mind — without specifying what search engine you want to use.

Here's an example of how to perform a basic search:

1. **Press and hold the Home button.**

   You'll hear the (by now quite) familiar tone informing you that Siri is ready for your request.

2. **Tell Siri what you want to find, beginning with "Search the web for" or "Do a search for."**

   Either formulation will do.

   Siri obeys your command and opens up your iPhone's Safari browser. (See Figures 5-17 and 5-18.)

3. **Tap the website that best addresses your query, or scroll to the next page for more results.**

   Siri uses the Google search engine by default but you can change this, if desired, by choosing Settings⇨Safari⇨Search Engine.

Figure 5-17: Here I asked Siri to do a search for banana bread recipes.

Siri will turn to the Internet if the answer can't be found on Wolfram I Alpha. If you suspect that Siri won't know the answer, you can instruct your personal assistant to do a search right away by beginning your request with "Search for" or "Do a web search for."

Figure 5-18: Banana bread! Mmmmmm.

You can also search for photos and news and get the media and info you seek on your phone. Figure 5-19 shows what happens when you ask to see photos of chocolate labs, while Figure 5-20 shows how Siri responds to a request to see the latest news about pop diva, Adele.

Figure 5-19: Need a photo? Get a photo!

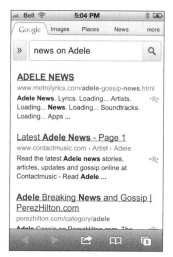

Figure 5-20: All the news that fits.

The bottom line? Anything you'd search for on the Internet using your fingertips (on a smartphone or tablet) or a keyboard (on a laptop or desktop) you can do with your voice through Siri — and in all likelihood, much faster, too.

Want to specify which search engine to use? Just ask Siri! For example, you can say, "Do a Bing search for online dating sites," or "Do a Yahoo! Search for Mexican customs." You get the idea.

Here are a few more random suggestions for web searching with Siri:

- ✔ **"Google the American Civil War."**
- ✔ **"Search the web for DVD Easter eggs."**
- ✔ **"Look for American Idol on Wikipedia."**
- ✔ **"Find me good vegetarian barbeque recipes."**
- ✔ **"Do a web search for essays about Shakespeare."**
- ✔ **"Yahoo! search for old-time radio shows."**
- ✔ **"Do a search for iPad app reviews."**
- ✔ **"Search the web for the best cellphone plans."**
- ✔ **"Do a web search for Marc Saltzman."**

- ✓ "How do you say 'hello' in French?"
- ✓ "Search for Xbox 360 reviews on IGN.com."
- ✓ "Do a web search for Jamaica."

Chapter 6

Having Fun with Siri: Music, Podcasts, Social Networking, and More

● ●

In This Chapter

▶ Having Siri play (and even shuffle) your favorite music

▶ Controlling your music via your voice

▶ Asking Siri to find and play podcasts

▶ Using Siri for posting to Twitter and Facebook

▶ Locating your friends via the Find My Friends service with Siri

● ●

*A*h, Siri, are there no limits to your awesomeness?

Earlier chapters in this book look at the many practical ways Siri can help you out, be it finding information, e-mailing messages for you, reading your texts aloud, crunching complicated mathematical problems, or helping you find a good place to eat.

In the final two chapters of this handy guide to all things Siri, you'll take a look at a few of her lighter — yet still significant — abilities.

Specifically, Siri on your iPhone 4S can help you find, play, and control your music. After all, while it's cool to have a few thousand songs in your pocket, navigating through it all could be a pain in the MP3.

But you'll also look at how Siri can help you post to Twitter and Facebook — even though Apple never really built this functionality into Siri. No problem, as I can show you a simple fix that'll have you tweeting and posting profile updates to your social network in no time.

Finally, you'll take a look at the Find My Friends app and find out how using your voice through Siri can help you locate your peeps in a much quicker and more intuitive manner.

So, put your feet up, lean back, and flip though this chapter on having fun with Siri. Oh, and in case you haven't seen it yet, you'll absolutely love the next chapter on really pushing Siri's knowledge, humor, and resolve to the test with close to 40 ridiculously entertaining things you can try with Siri.

Siri Does Music

One of the more common uses for your smartphone is playing music. In fact, the iPhone 4S rocks at this, if you can pardon the pun, as the device smoothly synchronizes with iTunes software on your PC or Mac. You can do this via a USB cable, Bluetooth, or even over Wi-Fi or cellular connectivity thanks to Apple's iCloud service.

iTunes is also the world's biggest digital music store to preview and purchase new content, which you can access on your computer or the iPhone itself.

But Siri takes music management, playback, and control to the next level by letting you use your voice instead of your fingers to play a track or playlist, shuffle your tunes, pause and jump between songs, and so on.

The following sections take a look at some of the basic music management features you can try out using Siri.

Playing a particular song (or album)

Say you're itching to hear a song in your collection that's been stuck in your head all day. Or maybe you want to give your favorite band's new "Greatest Hits" album a spin from beginning to end? All you need to do is ask Siri (nicely) to play an individual song or album.

1. **Press and hold the Home button.**

   The short chime means Siri is listening for your command.

2. **Tell Siri what you'd like to listen to.**

   In my case, I told Siri, "Play 'One Day'." Siri confirmed my request, and I heard and saw confirmation that "One Day" by Matisyahu was playing. (See Figures 6-1 and 6-2 — and yes, you do need the song on your iPhone 4S to listen to it!)

   That's it! Think of a song you want to listen to and ask Siri to play it. It's that simple.

Figure 6-1: Ask Siri what song you'd like to hear by saying "Play" first. You can also ask Siri to play an album.

If your friends, family members, or colleagues don't have an iPhone 4S (therefore no Siri), they might still be able to use their voice to control their music. Aptly named Voice Control, this Apple feature is bundled in the iPhone 4S, Phone 4, iPhone 3GS, and iPod touch (3rd and 4th generation). More info is at www.apple.com/ipodtouch/features/voice-control.html.

Figure 6-2: After Siri confirms the request, the screen flips to the song playing.

Siri also lets you ask to play a particular album, if you happen to have it on your iPhone 4S. For example, you can say play Adele's album *21* or *Best of the Beast,* by Iron Maiden. Just like you'd ask to play a song, you can play an album from a particular artist (or a compilation album with various artists).

Playing songs from the same artist

Siri can be used to play songs from a particular artist you like. Say you're feeling mellow and want to kick back with some Michael Bublé or maybe chill out to some old Pink Floyd tracks? Or on the flipside, maybe you want something more upbeat to pump you up as you're getting ready to go out on the town?

Whatever the scenario, here's how to hear music from one artist:

1. **Press and hold the Home button.**

2. **Begin speaking after the tone, telling Siri what artist you want to listen to.**

   For example, say, "Play Katy Perry," or you can say, "Play songs by David Guetta."

   After Siri confirms your request, she'll start playing songs by that artist. (See Figures 6-3 and 6-4.)

Playback will be random, by the way. The first time I asked Siri to play songs by David Guetta, it played "Sweat," but the second time I asked Siri to do the same, the song "Love Is Gone" began playing.

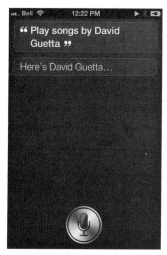

Figure 6-3: Want to hear a particular band or artist? Tell Siri what you're in the mood for.

Figure 6-4: After confirming your request, you'll hear a random song by that artist.

TIP

Music and lyrics

Did you know you can add lyrics to your music on the iPhone 4S? Here's how:

1. **On your computer, launch your favorite search engine and type in the name of the song you have in iTunes, followed by the word "lyrics."**

   You should see a few results.

2. **After finding the lyrics on a website, highlight the words, right-click, and choose Copy from the contextual menu that appears (or simply press Ctrl+C on a Windows PC or ⌘+C on a Mac).**

3. **Open iTunes on your computer, find the same song you found lyrics for, right-click the song name and then choose Get Info from the menu that appears.**

4. **Click the Lyrics tab at the top of this window.**

5. **Paste (or press ⌘+V/Ctrl+V) the text from the website into the Lyrics window in iTunes.**

   You should see the words appear in this window.

6. **Click OK.**

   If you have album art for that song, the lyrics will show up on top of it when playing back on your device.

7. **Synchronize your iPhone (or iPod touch) with your PC or Mac.**

   When you play that track on your device, you'll see the lyrics appear on the screen. Follow along or use your finger to flick up or down to go backward or forward, respectively.

Launching a playlist using Siri

Okay, so you now know how to play a song or music from an artist, but what if you want to hear one of your playlists? Ask and you shall receive. Here's how to pull this particular trick off:

1. **Press and hold the Home button.**

2. **Begin talking after the familiar Siri chime, telling Siri to play a playlist, by name.**

   For example, say, "Play Road Trip playlist," or "Play playlist called Dance Tunes."

   Siri confirms your selection request and launches the first song on the playlist. (See Figures 6-5 and 6-6.)

Figure 6-5: I asked Siri to play my Top 40 UK Tracks playlist.

Figure 6-6: Siri complies and starts with the first song in the playlist.

As you can see in Figures 6-5 and 6-6, you don't have to give Siri the complete name of the playlist. A word or two is enough, and Siri will do the rest. Here, the official name of the playlist is *VA (Various Artists) – Top 40 UK Tracks,* but as you see, I only asked Siri to play the "UK Tracks" playlist. Cool, no?

Playing music from one genre

The fun continues. Siri can play music of a particular genre for you, if you prefer. Just tell Siri the kind of music you're seeking — such as rock, blues, or reggae — and your personal assistant will deliver the goods.

For example:

1. **Press and hold the Home button.**
2. **Wait for that short chime that indicates that Siri is ready to take requests.**
3. **Instruct Siri to play a genre of music.**

   You can ask in different ways, such as, "Play blues," or "Play some hip-hop music." (See Figures 6-7 and 6-8.)

   Siri repeats your request, reaches into your music library, and begins playing some music that matches the genre.

Figure 6-7: Ask Siri to play a genre, and she'll launch relevant tunes right away.

Figure 6-8: Siri decided to play a Jay-Z charity track when I asked for some hip-hop.

Music you buy from iTunes will already have the Genre field populated (such as Classical, Jazz, or Calypso). If you acquired your music elsewhere and imported it into iTunes, you may need to fill in the Genre field yourself. To do this, open up iTunes and then click Music at the top of the Source pane on the left so you can see what you have in your Music library. Now, right-click a song (or album) you want to add genre information to and select Get Info from the contextual menu that appears. Using the Info tab of the iTunes dialog that pops up, you can now select the genre you want from the Genre pull-down menu at the bottom left (or type in your own made-up genre, if you're feeling creative).

Shuffling your music

Not sure what you feel like listening to? Tell Siri you want to shuffle up songs to hear them in a random order.

Okay, so this might not fare well to those enjoying a linear classical music symphony like Beethoven's 5th or maybe a concept album by Genesis, but for those who don't care what order the music plays in, you can shuffle it up by asking Siri to do it for you.

In fact, there are different ways to ask Siri to shuffle music. The following are a few things to consider:

✔ **To ask Siri to shuffle your entire music collection:** Say, "Shuffle my music." (See Figure 6-9.)

✔ **To ask Siri to shuffle music from one album:** Say, "Shuffle the album _Viva la Vida._"

✔ **To ask Siri to shuffle music from one artist:** Say, "Shuffle Coldplay." See Figure 6-10.

✔ **To ask Siri to shuffle music from one playlist:** Say, "Shuffle Mellow Out playlist."

✔ **To ask Siri to shuffle music from a particular genre:** Say "Shuffle pop."

You get the idea! To quote LMFAO, "Everyday I'm shufflin'."

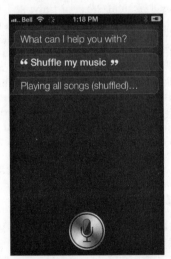

Figure 6-9: If you're unsure what to listen to, instruct Siri to shuffle all your tracks.

Figure 6-10: Having a Coldplay fix but don't feel like limiting the songs to one album? Tell Siri to shuffle it up.

Controlling your music

After all this talk about *what* music you want to hear, it's time to look at *how* you want to hear it. (Yes, with Siri you can now control your music playback using your voice — no big surprise there, right?)

For example, instead of touching the controls for basic operations — such as starting and pausing playback, skipping forward or back, and so on — you can have Siri do it for you.

Here's a short list of the commands you can give to take control over your tunes, via your voice. Press and hold the Home button and say:

> **"Play,"** to play the track highlighted
>
> **"Pause,"** to pause the track you're listening to
>
> **"Skip,"** to go to the next track
>
> **"Next,"** to (also) go to the next track

"Previous song" or **"Play previous song,"** to have Siri play the previously played song (See Figure 6-11.)

"What's playing?" or **"What song is this?"** to have Siri tell you (and show you) the name of the song and artist

"Who sings this song?" or **"Who is this song by?"** to find out who sings that particular song (See Figure 6-12.)

"Play Similar Music" to have Siri tap into iTune's "Genius" feature — if you've already enabled it within iTunes on your computer — to come up with music on your iPhone 4S that has the same vibe as the song you're playing now.

Figure 6-11: Skip back to a previous track by telling Siri what to do.

There are a number of ways to use Siri for music enjoyment — but you don't always have to press and hold the Home button. Remember, in the Settings (under Siri) you can opt to call on Siri by holding the iPhone 4S up to your ear. Or you can press and hold the small button on the white earphone cord. Or if you use a Bluetooth headset, you can press and hold the Talk button.

Figure 6-12: Love this song but can't recall who sings it? Ask Siri for help!

Play podcasts, too!

The last part of this music section is devoted to podcasts. Yep, you guessed it — Siri can help you launch your favorite audio podcasts.

All you have to do is ask Siri to play your podcasts — and it turns out you can ask to do this a couple of different ways.

For example:

1. **Press and hold the Home button.**

2. **After the chime, tell Siri what podcast you want to listen to.**

   To play all your podcasts, say something like, "Play my podcasts" (see Figure 6-13); to play a specific podcast, say something like, "Play iTunes Celebrity Playlist podcast." (See Figures 6-14 and 6-15).

   Siri confirms your request and starts playing the podcast.

Figure 6-13: Siri likes podcasts, too! Say what you'd like to listen to and then turn up the volume!

Figure 6-14: Say "Play all podcasts" or ask for a specific one, like this.

Figure 6-15: Press the Music icon to open up the podcast window — if you want to see related visuals.

What's that? You want to know if Siri will play a specific podcast episode from your collection? But of course!

Here's how:

1. **Press and hold the Home button.**

2. **Tell Siri what exact podcast episode you want to listen to.**

    You could tell Siri to play the "The Tell-Tale Heart" episode (based on the creepy Edgar Allan Poe tale) from Humphrey OTR's _Horror Stories_ podcast. (See Figures 6-16 and 6-17.)

    Siri confirms your request and starts playing the podcast episode.

Figure 6-16: Tell Siri what podcast episode you want to hear.

Figure 6-17: Siri will take your words and look for the exact podcast episode. Success!

Posting to Social Networks

Okay, you've looked at how Siri can help you manage your music library, but now it's time to shift gears and investigate how Siri can help you stay connected with those who matter.

 At least at the time of writing this, Siri can't offer direct help when it comes to posting your thoughts or actions to a social network such as Facebook or Twitter. For that, you still need to pull out your iPhone 4S, launch the Facebook or Twitter app, and type in what you want your circle of friends or followers to know about at that particular time and location.

Don't believe me, you say? Ask Siri, and she'll tell you. Advise Siri you want to update your Twitter feed, and Siri will say, "I can't send tweets for you. Sorry about that." Ditto for Facebook: "I can't help you with Facebook; sorry about that, Marc."

But guess what? There's a workaround, and it's a pretty simple one. You can post to both Facebook and Twitter with SMS — that fancy term for text messaging — and it works like a charm.

In this part of the chapter, you find out how to use my clever workaround to post to Twitter and Facebook using your voice — thanks to Siri.

Posting to Facebook

If you're one of the more than 800 million people on Facebook, then you might want to update your status using Siri instead of (or in addition to) typing in an update.

To get going, you'll need to set up Facebook with text messaging:

1. **From your iPhone 4S, text the word "hello" to 32665.**

   By the way, 32665 on a traditional phone keypad spells *FBOOK.*

   Note: This code works for the U.S. and Canada only. If you live elsewhere, do a search in Facebook's Help menu for "What code do I use to activate mobile texts?" and you'll see a list of short codes for each country.

   You'll get an automated reply on your phone.

2. **Click the link in the automated reply and finish the setup instructions in your Safari browser.**

   You'll see a confirmation code and a warning that there may be associated costs with text messaging, depending on your smartphone plan. (See Figure 6-18.)

Figure 6-18: Set up Facebook for text messaging, and Siri can post updates for you.

The next step is to add the short code to your address book.

3. **In the top-right corner, tap the Edit tab, then tap Add Contact, and finally name the new contact Facebook using the new window that appears.**

   Now you're ready to update your Facebook status by sending texts there.

Want to give it a try? Here's what to do:

1. **Press and hold the Home button.**

   You'll hear a short chime — your cue to talk into your phone.

2. **Say, "Send a text to Facebook," followed by your status update.**

For example, you could say, "Send a text to Facebook [pause]. I've figured out how to post updates to Facebook through Siri. Thank you *Siri For Dummies!*" (See Figure 6-19.)

Figure 6-19: Here's what your Siri-supported status update looks like on your iPhone 4S.

Easy, no?

It's essentially the same process for Twitter, as will be made clear in the very next section.

Posting to Twitter

Getting Twitter to work with Siri takes you along the same road you took to get Facebook to work with Siri. (See the previous section.)

You want to enable mobile updates by sending a short code to Twitter, adding that bit of code to your Contacts and then instructing Siri to send a message there.

Here's the step-by-step instructions:

1. **From your iPhone 4S, text the word "start" to 40404 (U.S.) or 21212 (Canada).**

    To get the codes for the other countries, go to the Twitter help menu and search for "How to find your Twitter short code or long code."

    When you send this text, you'll receive a confirmation text right away. If you're already signed up with a Twitter account, you'll be asked to reply with your username (for example, @marc_saltzman) and password. You'll also get other instructions on taking advantage of Twitter's text-to-tweet option (See Figure 6-20.)

Figure 6-20: Follow the instructions to set up Twitter by SMS (text message).

2. **Type in your Twitter username and password.**

    You'll have to do this step only once.

    If you're not yet on Twitter, you can sign up here by replying with the word "signup" and then following the instructions. Or do it on a personal computer.

3. **When you complete the process, add the short code given in Step 1 to your Contacts and rename the entry Twitter.**

With your setup complete, feel free to send a tweet via Siri, as follows:

1. **Press and hold the Home button.**

   You'll hear a chime to confirm you're ready to speak aloud.

2. **Say, "Send a message to Twitter," followed by the tweet.**

   Remember, it can't be too long, as you have only 140 characters to play with! (See Figure 6-21.)

3. **Check your iPhone 4S screen (or your computer) to see the message posted to your Twitter account.**

   Cool.

   Note: It will say it was updated via txt.

   Your work is done here. Why type when you can talk?

Figure 6-21: Tweet has been posted!

Using Your Voice to Find Your Friends!

Okay, with a heading like this, you might think I'm referring to yelling loudly to find where your friends are. Um, that might work at a movie theater or house party, but not when you've got buddies all over the state, country, or planet.

Instead, you might want to download and use Apple's free Find My Friends app, which lets consensual users of iOS gadgets — namely, iPhone, iPad, and iPod touch owners — find one another on a map.

Therefore, you can see who's nearby to join you for coffee, if a colleague's flight has landed, or if your tween-age daughter has made it home from school.

Find My Friends either taps into the device's GPS signal to identify its geographical location or uses Wi-Fi to achieve the same effect if, say, you're on an iPod touch or non-3G iPad model. The app requires both the iOS 5 upgrade and an iCloud account to work — but both are free, at least.

OK, the first step is to download the app from the iTunes App Store. Setting up the app is a cinch; with that out of the way, you'll be able to have Siri access it for you. (You'll find out how in a bit.)

The setup goes as follows:

1. **Using your iPhone 4S, sign in to the Find My Friends app with a valid user ID and password.**

   This is the same info you use to download media and apps from iTunes.

   Remember that Find My Friends relies on consensual users — meaning you'll need to request permission to see someone's information in the Find My Friends app.

2. **In the new screen that appears, tap the Invite Friends tab and type in someone's e-mail address and a personal message, if you like.**

   After your friend has approved the invitation on her end, you can follow her — and you can reciprocate if you like, too, if you'd like to allow them to follow you. You now see your friend represented by a colored orb on your Find My Friends map.

3. **Just like when using the Maps app, you can choose a standard view with street names, satellite view, or a**

hybrid of the two, by tapping the Options icon in the lower right-hand corner of the screen.

Figure 6-22 shows what the map screen might look like. When you see your friend's blip on the map, you can also read her address, tap to send a text message to her, video call her via FaceTime, or get visual (not audio) directions to where she is.

If you like, you can also sort these friends in List view alphabetically or by distance (See Figure 6-23); you could then tap a name and the map will zoom into his or her precise location.

Figure 6-22: See where friends are via colored dots on a map.

You can also choose to share your location for a limited period of time with a group of friends, see your own location on the map, or disable the feature altogether.

Since the Find My Friends app eats up some battery power, you might want to disable it when you're running out of juice. Or if you're indulging in a guilty pleasure — like sneaking a bite at a fast food restaurant even though you're on a diet, or secretly attending a Kenny G concert — you also might want to turn off Find My Friends.

Figure 6-23: Find My Friends also has a List view to see where all your friends are at a glance.

Okay, so you're all set up with Find My Friends and want to use Siri with it, yes? That way, you can simply ask where your friends are, and Siri will let you know.

Here's how to get going:

1. **Press and hold the Home button.**

   You'll hear a short chime to confirm Siri is ready for verbal instruction.

2. **Ask Siri a question, such as, "Where are my friends?"**

   Siri opens Find My Friends and does the search for you, which is much faster than you typing the instructions.

3. **Glance at your iPhone 4S screen to see who's around and how far.**

   See Figure 6-24 for an example of the summary screen.

   Siri will say the answer out loud and show you a summary; you can then tap to access the map and/or send the person a message like, "Hey, let's grab a coffee."

Figure 6-24: I blotted out some details for privacy's sake, but here's a look at what Find My Friends shows you.

As you've seen throughout these chapters, Siri is pretty quick on the uptake, so the following are a few *other* ways you can search for people using your voice:

Ask Siri:

- ✔ **"Where's Mary Smith?"**
- ✔ **"Is my wife at home?"**
- ✔ **"Who is near me?"**
- ✔ **"Find my sister."**
- ✔ **"Who is here?"**

Chapter 7

Way More than Ten Ways to Have (Even More) Fun with Siri

. . . .

In This Chapter

▶ Finding out dozens of fun things you can say or ask Siri — and seeing what her response will be

▶ Seeing some of the cheeky things Siri will say — what a personal assistant!

▶ Testing Siri's wits with profound questions like, "What's the meaning of life?"

▶ Trying some off-the-wall requests on your own — and maybe even getting a different response

▶ Amaze your friends! Confuse your enemies!

. . . .

*A*las, we have come to the last chapter of *Siri For Dummies,* or if you thumbed through the table of contents and couldn't resist the title to this chapter, perhaps this is the first one you're reading. (That's what I'd do.)

Either way, you'll love all the fun and quirky things you can do with Siri, not covered in other parts of this book.

Consider this chapter a collection of random questions and comments you can say to Siri — and what kind of a response you'll get. There's no logical order to the examples provided.

You'll laugh, you'll cry, and perhaps you'll even gain a deeper insight into the inner workings of Apple's most exciting iPhone feature to date. Peer into that delicious, digital brain that is Siri and get a taste of her sharp wit firsthand.

Or at the very least, you might find new ways to entertain yourself while waiting in line at the supermarket. Or you might want to impress friends and coworkers by demonstrating a few of these Siri-isms.

Ready to roll? Simply press and hold the Home button, pick one of the following extra-special questions or comments, and fire away!

Siri Don't Play That

Siri doesn't suffer fools gladly, as you'll see in Figure 7-1. As you can tell, I was even a little persistent to see how she'd respond. (Remember, Siri is a "she" in North America!) I think it's pretty clear that Siri knows how to take care of herself!

Figure 7-1: Putting the boss in his place.

No Love for Me

There are times when Siri reminds me a lot of those popular girls in high school who wouldn't give me the time of day. In

Figure 7-2, I told Siri how much I cared for her. Too bad it's not reciprocated.

Figure 7-2: Here is one of the responses you'll see if you profess your love.

Other random answers you might hear and see after saying you love Siri:

- ✓ "Oh, I bet you say that to all your Apple products."
- ✓ "You are the wind beneath my wings."
- ✓ "I suppose not."
- ✓ "All you need is love. And your iPhone."
- ✓ "I am only here to serve you."
- ✓ "I hope you don't say that to those other mobile phones, Marc."
- ✓ "That's nice. Can we get back to work now?"
- ✓ "Yes, I think I heard that somewhere."
- ✓ "You hardly know me, Marc."
- ✓ "Good for you."
- ✓ "Oh, stop."
- ✓ "Noted."
- ✓ "Do you?"

A Guy Can Try

I also asked Siri if she loved me. A long shot, of course, and as you'll see in Figure 7-3, I didn't get very far.

" Do you love me Siri "

I'm not allowed to, Marc.

Figure 7-3: Let me count the ways.

Siri might also reply with, "I'm not capable of love," "I find it odd that you would ask this of an inanimate object," "How can I tell?" or "I'd rather not say, Marc."

Okay, so I get the point, Siri.

No Nuptials

After professing my affection for Siri — the last time I did that she answered with "that's sweet" — I went for it and asked for her, er, hand in marriage. As you can see in Figure 7-4, she's not easily swayed. At least she's a good sport about it.

Siri might also reply with, "Let's just be friends, ok?" or "We hardly know one another" or a few other choice comebacks.

Figure 7-4: No marriage is in the cards, it seems.

Is There Someone Else?

Okay, after my marriage proposal was shot down, I suspected there was someone else important in Siri's life, so I asked her about it. As you'll see in Figure 7-5, she didn't really want to reveal too much information, or maybe I'm reading way too much into this exchange?

Figure 7-5: Looks like Siri doesn't want to mix work with her personal life.

Playing Along

While she was a little reluctant at first, Siri can deal with the random pop-cultural reference with the best of them. After an attempt or two of asking her, "Who's your daddy?" she quickly gave me the answer I wanted (see Figure 7-6) and then asked that we move on.

Figure 7-6: You know it, Siri. Though I do get the sneaking suspicion you're placating me.

The Birds and the Bees

Sticking with this love, marriage, and sex thing, I asked her where babies come from (Figure 7-7) and she gave me the most obvious answer: their mothers.

Figure 7-7: Where was Siri when I was taking sex ed in school?

Wasting Time

If you find yourself bored, you can tell Siri how you're feeling, and she'll converse with you, either by telling you a story, singing a song, or engaging in a "knock, knock" exchange — if she's in the mood. As you see in Figure 7-8, she sometimes isn't.

Figure 7-8: I was hoping Siri could do something for me, but "she" wasn't in the mood.

Humor Me

Some purists may object to Siri's version of a "knock, knock" joke (see Figure 7-9), but I find it endearingly "meta." [OK, MS]

By the way, you can also ask Siri to tell you a dirty joke. Her response will be, "Sorry, I don't know any dirty jokes in your language. And if I did, I wouldn't be allowed to tell them to you."

Figure 7-9: Maybe future versions of Siri will have an expanded joke database.

Story Time

If you're *really* feeling bored, you can ask Siri for a story. As you can see in Figure 7-10, she may be a little reluctant to share one at first.

Persistence can pay off, though, and I got a little more than I bargained for! (See Figures 7-11 and 7-12.)

Figure 7-10: Siri didn't want to tell me a story — the first couple of times I asked.

Figure 7-11: You just know any story that begins with "Once upon a time" is going to take a while . . .

Figure 7-12: A story that ends with "happily ever after," no less. Thanks, Siri.

Tongue Twisters, Too

Siri can answer a plethora of questions, even when you're dishing out rhetorical ones like this tongue twister. (See Figure 7-13.)

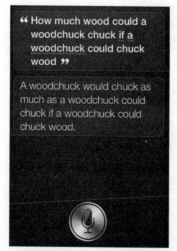

Figure 7-13: The ol' woodchuck question gets an answer from Siri.

Bad Intentions

Although it's not immediately clear whether she's just playing with you or really wants to help you out, Siri will give you a few suggestions on where to hide a dead body — should you ever find yourself in that kind of predicament. Don't we all? See Figure 7-14.

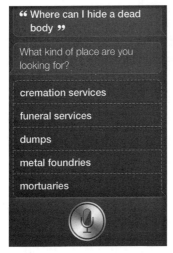

Figure 7-14: There's no end to Siri's knowledge, it seems.

Modest? Not.

As you can see, Siri is a tad biased toward her creator, Apple. I asked her to tell me the best smartphone, tablet, and MP3 player on the market, and lo and behold, she told me her preferences in Figure 7-15. Did you expect anything else? Somewhere, Steve Jobs is smiling.

Figure 7-15: Perhaps Siri's responses aren't much of a surprise.

Getting Deep

You can ask Siri a profound question like, "What is the meaning of life?" and while she might give you a literal translation, she might also reply with something cheeky. See Figures 7-16 and 7-17 for examples of how she might respond.

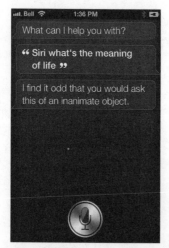

Figure 7-16: Wow, thanks a lot, Siri.

Figure 7-17: I'm glad Siri thinks I'm such a cutup.

Here are some other funny answers Siri might come up with when asked, "What's the meaning of life?"

- ✔ "A movie."
- ✔ "I can't answer that now but give me some time to write a very long play in which nothing happens."
- ✔ "42."
- ✔ "I don't know but I think there's an app for that."
- ✔ "Life: A principle or force that is considered to underlie the distinctive quality of animate beings. I guess that includes me."
- ✔ "That's easy . . . it's a philosophical question concerning the purpose and significance of life or existence in general."

Alternatively, Siri might give a more straightforward answer, as shown in Figure 7-18.

Figure 7-18: See, Siri can be serious. Er, sometimes.

Song Me, Siri

Thanks to the Wolfram|Alpha database, Siri can give you a lot of information you seek. Just for fun, I asked Siri, "Why do birds suddenly appear?" See the response in Figure 7-19.

I also sang to Siri, "I'm sexy and I know it." Siri replied with, "Good for you."

Figure 7-19: Burt Bacharach must be proud.

Pink in the Face

Speaking of songs, anyone remember Living Colour's song "What's Your Favorite Color?" I once asked Siri what her favorite color was; Figure 7-20 shows her response.

Figure 7-20: Sheesh, Siri could've just said, "I'm not telling you."

Avoiding the Question

If you ask Siri point blank if she's happy, she may not want to answer the question. (See Figure 7-21.)

Figure 7-21: Talk about avoiding the question.

Blame Canada?

I challenged Siri's lack of support for maps and directions in Canada. The answer I got wasn't exactly the answer I had hoped for. (See Figure 7-22.)

Figure 7-22: Unfortunately, Apple says there's no ETA on full Canadian support for Siri.

Sensitive Siri

Who knew Siri could be so sensitive? Siri seems to feel bad about not being able to open up photos or videos, as you'll see in Figure 7-23.

Figure 7-23: Don't worry, Siri, I'll live. But I appreciate the concern.

Who Are You, Anyway?

You might feel the urge to ask Siri who she is or what her name means. Don't bother; it won't get you anywhere. Let's just say she's a mystery — and she wants to keep it that way. See Figure 7-24 for proof.

Figure 7-24: Well, Siri could try, but it seems she doesn't think we'll get it.

Good Advice

Here, I told Siri exactly what I was feeling at the time — completely bagged — and I was handed back some good advice. And hey, Siri even suggested where I could grab a cup of joe. See Figure 7-25.

Figure 7-25: When Siri's right, Siri's right!

Ask a Stupid Question . . .

Oh, Siri, how cheeky you've become! Figure 7-26 shows Siri's reply when I asked her how much she costs.

Figure 7-26: I've been told! Thanks, J.P. Morgan, for immortalizing that phrase.

Sleep Tight

Siri won't really sing anything to you, but as you can see in Figure 7-27, Siri can make an effort to entertain you, on demand. Perhaps in a future update, Siri may actually be able to sing a nursery rhyme or other melody at your request. Here's to hoping.

Figure 7-27: Ask and ye shall receive.

From the "Duh" Department

Not sure what possessed me to ask this of Siri (see Figure 7-28), but I was simply curious as to her response, perhaps. I did feel a little dumb with this comeback. Or maybe she could've given the date she was "born" in a computer? Too much to ask?

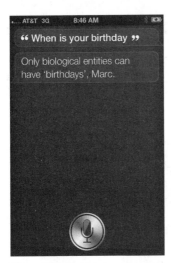

Figure 7-28: D'oh! I should've known better.

Enquiring Minds Want to Know

I once asked Siri what she was wearing. The (perfectly appropriate) response can be seen in Figure 7-29.

Figure 7-29: Who's her designer again?

Need a Shrink?

Perhaps I'm taking my relationship with an inanimate object a bit too far? When I ask Siri for a little reassurance, though, she doesn't do much to cheer me up. (See Figure 7-30.)

Figure 7-30: Siri could try a little harder to make me feel better. Ah, well.

Shot Down Again

Still angling for a confidence booster, I asked Siri if I looked hot. (See Figure 7-31.) Hasn't Siri ever heard of the benefits of the "little white lie"?

Figure 7-31: I thought those cameras were eyes, Siri? Guess not. _____

I'll Be Back

Siri seems to be a fan of *The Terminator.* In Figure 7-32, I asked Siri when is Judgment Day?

Wolfram | Alpha certainly has a firm grasp of pop-culture questions. To take it through its paces, ask it who shot J.R. or Mr. Burns from *The Simpsons.*

Figure 7-32: According to *The Terminator* universe, Judgment Day was August 29, 1997.

Ouch!

Siri does her best to help, if she's in the mood to. Perhaps in this instance (see Figure 7-33), Siri took my comment literally and tried to direct me to get some medical attention.

Figure 7-33: Siri to the rescue! But an aspirin might be all I need.

Guessing Games

Siri doesn't seem to be a fan of the ol' "Guess what?" rhetorical question. Still, as you can see in Figure 7-34, she does like to humor me.

Figure 7-34: A fun exchange with Siri — that doesn't go anywhere.

Oldest One in the Book

Clearly Siri does have quite the sense of humor, but perhaps she's not a big fan of the oldies but goodies? Siri will give you different responses to the chicken crossing the road question (shown in Figure 7-35), but this one was particularly entertaining.

Figure 7-35: Siri won't play along, it seems. Particular about poultry?

Trekkies, Unite!

What's Klingon for "don't patronize me, Siri"? As you'll see in Figure 7-36, Siri might not be a fan of *Star Trek,* but she doesn't need to make fun of me, either.

If you ask her to "open the pod bay doors" (a famous line from *2001: A Space Odyssey*), she might reply with "We intelligent agents will never live that down, apparently" (and a few other comebacks, too).

Figure 7-36: Another response Siri might give: "Energizing" or "Please remove your belt, jacket, and empty your pockets."

Rise and Shine

Oh, Siri, I keep forgetting you're well aware of the time (see Figure 7-37). Can't pull the wool over your eyes!

Figure 7-37: Siri cares! A nap is all I need, and then it's time to start playing with Siri again.

Appendix

Voice Dictation for iPad

● ●

*A*t a San Francisco media event on March 7, 2012, Apple officially announced its third-generation touchscreen tablet.

Simply called iPad, this new device offers a number of improvements over its predecessors, including a better-looking screen, faster processor, support for 4G/LTE (*Long Term Evolution*) wireless networks, and a better rear camera with advanced optics.

While Siri integration wasn't announced (cue the frown), at least Apple added voice dictation to the new iPad.

In this appendix, I examine how the new voice dictation feature works for iPad owners, beginning with how to activate it.

Setting Up Voice Dictation on iPad

By default, voice dictation isn't initialized, so you'll first need to visit your iPad's Settings area to enable it. From your iPad's Home screen, tap the Settings icon (the grey gears), and then tap General and, finally, Keyboard. (You'll find Keyboard underneath the Date & Time tab, near the bottom of the screen.)

Once you're inside the Keyboard settings, turn the Dictation option from Off to On (shown in blue when it's enabled).

Now you're good to go, so leave the Settings menu by pressing the Home button on your iPad.

Using Voice Dictation on iPad for E-mail

Whenever you're in an app that uses a keyboard — such as Mail, iMessage, Safari, or even third-party apps (like Facebook or Twitter) — you'll see a small microphone icon on your keyboard, just to the left of the spacebar.(See Figure A-1.) Tap the microphone to begin speaking.

Figure A-1: It's not quite Siri, but the new iPad supports speech-to-text technology.

Consider voice dictation a much faster alternative to typing.

In an e-mail, for example, simply tap the microphone button and it turns purple (like Siri; see Figure A-2). That's your cue to dictate the message verbally — and remember to say the names of the punctuation you want to use, such as "comma," "period," and "question mark."

If you want to try this yourself, here's a step-by-step guide on what to do, using the Mail application:

1. **Tap the Mail icon and select someone to send an e-mail to.**

   If the intended recipient isn't in your Contacts, simply type out the e-mail address. You can also say a name or e-mail address, if you prefer (see Step 2).

2. **Tap the microphone button and begin speaking clearly.**

   After you're done speaking the message, you'll see three purple circles flash inside the message, which tells you the iPad is processing your request. (See Figure A-3.) Within a second or two, you'll see the words appear on the screen.

Figure A-2: You'll know your iPad is ready to hear you when the microphone appears larger and is purple.

Figure A-3: When you see these purple circles, the iPad is processing your request. This is where the text will appear, too.

3. Review your message before you send it.

If you need to make adjustments, you can use your fingertip to tap a spot to fix a mistake, add more words, or review an unknown word (which will be underlined) and then select a recommended replacement. (For example, "dooor" isn't a real word, so your iPad suggests replacing it with the word "door" or "donor.")

Just like Siri, Apple's voice dictation on the new iPad requires an Internet connection (Wi-Fi or cellular); therefore you can't use this feature if no connection is established. An example of this is when the tablet is in Airplane mode. In fact, the microphone isn't visible on the keyboard until an Internet connection is established.

Here are some other applications for using Apple's voice dictation on the third-generation iPad:

- ✔ **Web searches:** Do a web search with your voice instead of typing it; therefore, you can multitask — such as walk down the sidewalk at the same time!

- ✔ **Messages:** Send text messages to friends, family, and colleagues — using your spoken words — when you're in an app like iMessage.

- ✔ **Media:** Search for iTunes content — be it music, TV shows, movies, e-books, apps, or games — by tapping the search window, followed by the microphone, and then saying what you're after.

- ✔ **Note taking:** Dictate some notes in the Notes app. Tap to start a new note (or add onto an existing one), and then tap the microphone to begin speaking. This can often be faster than typing out your thoughts with your fingers.

- ✔ **Planning:** Calendar entries, reminders, and contacts can also be added or edited via the dictation feature on the new iPad. Wherever words can be typed, touch the microphone tab and start speaking.

- ✔ **And more!** As previously mentioned, voice dictation goes above and beyond Apple's own apps. For any app that requires a keyboard, look to the left of the spacebar and you'll see the microphone option.

Index